WESTERN
HIGHLANDS

1 Liathach from stream near Loch Torridon

WESTERN HIGHLANDS

By

ARTHUR GARDNER, M.A., F.S.A.

Author of *Peaks, Lochs, and Coasts of the Western Highlands*; *Sun, Cloud, and Snow in the Western Highlands*; *The Art and Sport of Alpine Photography*; *An Introduction to French Church Architecture*; *A Handbook of English Medieval Sculpture*; *Medieval Sculpture in France*; *Alabaster Tombs*

Illustrated by
300 Photographs mostly by the Author
Second Edition, revised

B. T. BATSFORD LTD.

LONDON   *   NEW YORK
TORONTO   SYDNEY

First published in present form Summer 1947
Second Edition, revised, 1948

MADE AND PRINTED IN GREAT BRITAIN
BY JARROLD AND SONS LTD., NORWICH FOR THE PUBLISHERS B. T. BATSFORD LTD.,
LONDON: 15 NORTH AUDLEY STREET, W.I AND MALVERN WELLS, WORCESTERSHIRE
NEW YORK: 122 EAST 55TH STREET   TORONTO: 480–6 UNIVERSITY AVENUE
SYDNEY: 156 CASTLEREAGH STREET

CONTENTS

PREFACE

My two books, *The Peaks, Lochs, and Coasts of the Western Highlands*, and *Sun, Cloud, and Snow in the Western Highlands* have now been out of print for several years. The kind reception given to them, and especially to the first, has suggested to me that a new edition might be acceptable. With this in view I have thought it best to amalgamate the two and to add a page or two here, a paragraph there, and a couple of chapters to fill some important gaps, and thus to make my survey much more complete and comprehensive. At the same time the original idea remains to give a general impression of what the country is like rather than detailed instructions as to how to visit it. It does not pretend to compete with the various guide-books but to supplement them by attracting notice to its peculiar charms and providing an illustrated record which may serve to recall the joys of a holiday among the mountains. For a detailed description of the individual hills and the walks and climbs they provide the reader must be referred to the admirable series of guides published by the Scottish Mountaineering Club.

The War is going to make great changes in our outlook and surroundings, and the Highlands are threatened with development schemes, such as the hydro-electric plans or vast forestry extensions, which may alter the face of the country to a considerable extent. If the tourist industry is to be worked up there will have to be new roads, new hotels, and new ways of access. It will not, therefore, be possible for a single individual to go over all the stage again, especially when increasing years deprive one of some of the elasticity of youth. My descriptions, therefore, must be of the Western Highlands as they were between the two great wars, and if they fail to give an altogether up-to-date lead to the intending visitor, they may at least have an archaeological value as giving a picture of what the country was like at that time.

The new edition has a fair number of new illustrations, and I have decided to strengthen the photographic gallery by introducing sixteen examples from the collection of my brother Hugh Gardner (Figs. 8, 128, 150, 152, 153, 158, 161, 163, 164, 165, 173, 175, 187, 194, 202 and 224), whose early death at the age of fifty has deprived me of a companion who could sympathize with all my foibles and enthusiasms, and the mountains of a lifelong devotee and advocate. Several of these were taken from the mountain-tops during recent years when my older legs were beginning to shy at the steeper slopes. Many of the tramps described in the book were done in his company, and these few pictures may serve as a small tribute to his memory.

PREFACE TO THE SECOND EDITION

Difficulties and shortages in the printing and binding trades have caused a considerable time to elapse since the first edition of this book was prepared for press. During that time developments have taken place in the Highlands which may render obsolete some of the comments or descriptions in the present volume. Work has begun on four or five hydro-electric schemes which will alter the face of the country, not without much damage to its amenities. The most damaging of these is that in Glen Affric and Glen Cannich, which have been designated as one of the proposed national parks. Protests from nature-lovers have caused some modification of the original plans, and Loch Affric itself may be spared with its ancient pine forests, but Loch Beneveian and Loch Mullardoch in Glen Cannich will be converted into reservoirs with huge dams and destruction of their natural shores. So far Strath Farrar seems to have been spared.

The Loch Sloy Scheme is less disastrous, as the loch is seldom visited and is so high up that its shores would be rather bleak anyhow. Here the amount of damage will depend upon the design and siting of the power house on Loch Lomond. The northern scheme is also away from the very finest Scenery, and Loch Fannich is also so high up that its banks are wild rather than lovely. The smaller project ar Morar will destroy a lovely little salmon river, but the damage will be restricted to a comparatively small area.

The old plan to tap Loch Quoich and Glen Garry which was twice rejected by Parliament has not yet been revived, but if it is it should be opposed by all lovers of the finest scenery in Scotland.

The Tummel-Tay project, being nearer to more populous areas, seems likely to very detrimental to a favourite tourist neighbourhood, but is rather outside the country to which this volume is dedicated.

The report of the National Parks Committee for Scotland has also appeared (late 1947). To lovers of unspoilt nature it is rather a disappointing document compared with the excellent report on the same subject for England and Wales. It suggests the purchase outright of five parks and sets out a scheme for developing them with more emphasis on the need for building up a successful tourist industry than on the conservation of nature unadorned. It takes for granted the abominations of the hydro-electric engineers even in the national parks themselves and is grateful to them for improving roads and erecting huge dams which might prove objects of interest to visitors! It concludes by a plan for developing the Glen Affric National Park which suggests a kind of refined Butlin camp with community centres, pony stables, caravan camps, garages, youth hostels, hotels, school, workshops, shops, tea rooms, etc., etc. There would be houses and offices for the hydro-electric and forestry workers who would apparently be engaged on destroying the wild natural beauties to which the district owes its charm. It is perhaps fortunate that some other areas like that round the great sea lochs recommended for conservation in this volume have been omitted from this list so that they may look to their remoteness and inaccessibility to preserve them until a more enlightened policy is adopted. The best hope for them, as also for the Cuillin hills of Skye, might be to fall eventually into the hands of the National Trust.

This is a depressing note on which to conclude, but it may render this volume greater value as a description of what the country was like between the two world wars and before the hand of the despoiler was let loose upon it.

ARTHUR GARDNER

March 1948

2 Cloudscape from Strontian

3 Cul Mòr from Canisp

I   *Introduction*

It is a rash proceeding for a mere Englishman to attempt to write a book about the Highlands, but I hope those better qualified to do so will pardon my presumption if I can show a genuine love for the wild hills and lochs of the north—a feeling with which the true-born Scot must always sympathize.

So many books have been written about the mountains that perhaps some excuse is needed for adding yet another to the number, especially as I can make no claim for the present volume as a contribution to scientific knowledge, or even as a record of adventure. It is not a guide-book, but is meant more as a supplement to the guide-books, supplying just those things which that most business-like form of literature does not give. It is designed as a pictorial record of some of the most characteristic types of Highland scenery on a new plan, making its appeal especially to the eye by means of the photographs which are the *raison d'être* of the book, and accompanying them by just so much text as will explain the points they are intended to bring out, and describe the conditions under which they were taken.

Long and flowery descriptions of scenery are apt to be boring, and it is better to let the face of nature speak for itself in the pictures, and to add only such details as anyone turning over the pages will want to know, or to reinforce the impression by a few words where the camera fails to do more than hint at the splendour of nature's noblest efforts.

Roughly speaking, visitors to the Highlands may be divided into five categories. The first is composed of the cragsmen or climbers, men of iron nerve and tireless energy, who seek excitement in scaling pinnacles and chimneys, and despise the poor foot-slogger who climbs his mountain by the obvious route. The second class is made up of more ordinary people, who are content to enjoy the beauties of nature from a more or less safe standpoint; who do not mind a reasonably long tramp over rough country, but do not hesitate to gain the best viewpoint by the easy way. My third class consists of the sportsmen—deer stalkers, grouse shooters, and fishermen—to whom the hills and streams are pleasant accessories rather than the main objectives of their visit. The fourth is made up of the ordinary tourist, who goes by the usual stock routes, inspects the regular show places, but has not enough initiative to plan out trips for himself. The fifth and last is the unspeakable class of tripper who scatters orange peel and sandwich papers in show places, and whose object is to let off his animal spirits in noise and vulgarity. Fortunately the last do not penetrate far into the Highlands where the inhabitant, whatever his shortcomings, is a born gentleman.

From the above remarks the reader will no doubt have guessed that the writer of this book belongs to class two. It is from the point of view of the rambler rather than that of the climber that the subject will be approached in this volume. It is written mainly for those who love to tramp for miles over the hills, to search out the finest scenes by silent lake or roaring torrent, in wooded glen or wave-swept shore, or to worship in the solitude of the mountain-top, and wonder at the wild splendour of crag and precipice in nature's sternest retreats.

Lovers of nature will, it is hoped, find some suggestions for future exploration in its pages, and a record of memorable scenes to take home with them after a holiday, and perhaps the Scotsman living far from his native home may value a pictorial record of the hills and glens among which he was born or spent his youthful days.

Even the climber, should he find the text dull and lacking in excitement, may enjoy photographs of the scenes amid which he has spent many a happy holiday, for Ruskin's greased-pole acrobat is happily rare among real cragsmen, and the majority of those who take up this strenuous form of exercise have done so because it brings them into touch with nature in its grandest and wildest forms.

To some men the savage and the sublime seem to offer a challenge to measure their own skill and endurance against the resistance of frowning precipice and dizzy ledge, and the joy of triumph after a successful climb is a feeling with which those can sympathize to whom a spice of danger adds not pleasure but anxiety, and whose more placid temperament is content with the vision of beauty attained by reasonable effort and no undue risk to life and limb. The climber, too, in return may feel some bond of sympathy with his less ambitious friend if the latter really loves the mountains. And, as climbers sometimes grow old, or marry anxious wives, even they may in later life enjoy the kind of tramp described in this volume, and may be glad to have in it some pictured memories of pleasant days among the hills.

With the sportsman we have a bone to pick later on, but for the tourist, using the word in the narrow sense explained above, we have more hope. He is not often found north of the Caledonian Canal, and abounds chiefly along the steamer routes, and the more accessible country in the south and west. The first chapter will therefore appeal most to him, but perhaps the perusal of these pages will tempt him to venture farther afield, and to aspire to a more honourable place in our second category.

It is, indeed, one of the main objects of the book to show what a magnificent holiday playground exists in the north and west for our people jaded by the rush and complications of modern life. It is not generally recognized what a superb stretch of country is lying at our doors, and those who have already found it out would welcome other kindred spirits to share their quiet pleasures, and would not be sorry to see some improvement in accommodation and means of access, which could easily be made without importing any of the

4 Sgùrr-nan-Ceathreamhnan from Sgùman Còinntich

5 Skye from Sgùman Còinntich

turmoil of modern life, from which we should like to preserve this region as a sanctuary for ever.

This will, I am afraid, exclude the interests of our fifth class, the tripper, but his outlook and sympathies are so different from the rest that it is impossible to cater for him here.

And now for the sportsman! With the fisherman we have no quarrel. His conversation may at times become tedious to those who do not share his tastes, and he is always praying for the type of weather that other people do not want, but he helps to support the right sort of inn in the remoter districts, and may find here and there in these pages a picture of some loch beside which he has spent happy hours, for the patient waiting required by his pursuit must give plenty of opportunity for the quiet contemplation of the lovely scenes around him.

It is different, however, with the deer stalker. He is rich and powerful, and has sought to make the whole of the north into a private enclosure, from which not only the lovers of nature should be excluded, but even the natives whose forefathers have dwelt there for centuries should be driven out.

In the old days when the Highland chieftain dwelt among his tenants it might have seemed presumptuous for the stranger to raise a protest against exclusion, but now that the chiefs have mostly been driven by excessive taxation to let or sell their rights to the American millionaire or the war profiteer, we have to face a different problem. A new purse-proud owner is more difficult to deal with than the old laird with his ancient tradition of service to those about him in return for his position and rights. In a recent book,[1] Dr. E. A. Baker has attracted much attention by his strong protest against the present state of affairs under which individuals can appropriate vast tracts of country to their own exclusive use, and can make them practically inaccessible, in spite of rights-of-way, by letting roads and bridges fall into disrepair, and by closing the only inns or places of refreshment which in former days made visits to such places possible. He puts forth a strong plea for better access to what ought to be a national sports ground, in which there is ample room for the lovers of wild nature and solitude to find that spiritual refreshment so much needed to-day.

It is not necessary to repeat Dr. Baker's arguments here, but I should like to take this opportunity to associate myself with him in his protest. That one-fifth of the whole surface of Scotland should be given up to private deer forests is surely a scandal that needs to be dealt with, and though I have personally been little interfered with in the early spring, when no harm could possibly be done to sporting interests, most people are only able to take their holidays in summer or autumn and the closing of inns is a real grievance.

Economically it cannot be sound to devote so much territory to provide a few weeks' sport for the favoured few. Deer are destructive beasts and destroy the native forests by eating the young trees; they support fewer men than their predecessors the sheep, and venison, except in the eyes of those who have shot it, is a poor substitute for mutton. Hunting is a primitive

[1] *The Highlands with Rope and Rucksack*, by E. A. Baker, D.Litt., M.A. (Witherby, 1923).

instinct of man, and no doubt there is a certain excitement in stalking an elusive beast like the deer, but modern weapons of precision, and skilful beaters, often reduce this so-called sport to a mere butchery, and it can hardly be argued that the slaughter of a noble animal is such a refining pastime for the great ones of the earth that it is worth while to devote so large a portion of the country to such a purpose, or to depopulate glens which once supported a happy and prosperous population, and to shut out thousands who are yearning for the peace and solitude which only a mountain country can give.

Economic pressure and the high taxation resulting from a second World War may help to settle this question of the deer forests, as there may be few men left rich enough to monopolize this expensive form of sport. Many proposals have been put forward to restore prosperity to the Highlands, but the question is too big to be dealt with here, and we shall have to confine our remarks to those points which will have most effect on the scenery of the country. Where there is sufficient feed it would be an excellent thing to replace the deer by sheep. The demand for home-grown mutton and wool is likely to increase, and the presence of sheep on the hills does not necessitate the exclusion of the rambler or tourist at any time of the year so long as he closes gates after him and keeps dogs under control. The farmers of the English Lake District and North Wales have found this a valuable resource, and though the snow may lie longer on the higher hills of the north there must be much country suitable for such a purpose.

Local industries, like the production of home-spun cloth, could be extended to supplement farming operations, but the old crofters could hardly be expected to return to the primitive conditions under which they lived before the bad days of expulsion and emigration. A big expansion of the tourist industry brings, perhaps, the most hopeful prospects, and with the higher wages likely after the war and wider distribution of wealth, the need for holiday resorts is likely to expand. The region within reach of the Clyde will no doubt continue to cater for those who like to go about in droves and seek mass-produced entertainment, but those who wish for quiet commune with nature could be provided for in the magnificent country of the west and north.

Means of access would have to be improved, new roads planned and footpaths improved, and new hotels and youth hostels placed in suitable positions. What is really wanted will be inexpensive inns on the lines of Swiss mountain hotels, providing comfort without luxury and necessities without display. The Swiss seem able to provide all that is wanted in the way of provisions and all other tourist requisites in places far more inaccessible than anything in Scotland, thousands of feet above the sea, served only by mountain tracks where the only transport is by mule or the backs of men. Inns established in ideal positions at the head of the great sea lochs could be served by boat, and there should be plenty of small naval craft after the war available for such a purpose.

But if the tourist industry is to flourish steps must be taken to preserve the beauty of the country and to protect it from commercial spoliation. Quarrying should be controlled and ambitious schemes for developing water power should be closely watched. Beauty is an asset of enormous commercial value, and once destroyed can never be restored. Country planning committees should bear this in mind, especially in selecting sites for future national parks. Even remote areas which might be suitable for such a purpose as means of access improve with the advancing years should be given protection, even if not immediately required. The Glasgow Corporation has destroyed the famous silver strand on Loch Katrine, and a sort of concrete parade now replaces the lovely natural banks of that once beautiful loch, the British Aluminium Company has created hideous smoky factories at Kinlochleven and Banavie, and the wild charms of the Tummel have been sacrificed to a hydro-electric scheme. We cannot afford to go on fouling our own nest in this way for the sake of short-sighted financial gains, and we should look upon ourselves as trustees of this natural heritage of beauty to be preserved, even at great cost, for the generations yet to come. The new Government hydro-electric schemes seem bound to do irreparable damage to some of the finest parts of the Highlands if not closely watched. Unless the amenity committee, inserted in the bill as a sop to the critics, has real power to forbid whole development plans, any grandiose scheme for building huge dams and raising the level of lakes must do damage to the scenery which no tinkering or modifications of details can disguise. Why should we spend millions of money in this way when it has yet to be proved that power cannot be produced more cheaply on the coalfields if proper allowance for costs of installation of the water-power is made and when in a few years the development of atomic power may render all this plant obsolete? Labour would have to be imported temporarily, and when the damage has been done very few men would be required for maintenance, and the only people to have benefited would be the big contractors. The Association for the Preservation of Rural Scotland has ideas for promoting a number of small and inconspicuous plants which could supply all local demands for light and power without serious harm to the amenities. We should do more good to the real interests of the Highlands by spending three millions in this way than by using the thirty millions Parliament has been rash enough to place at the disposal of the spoilers.

The only real security that can be given is by segregating some of the finest tracts of country as national parks, in which the preservation of natural features would be the first consideration. What a magnificent site, for example, for such a national park could be found in such an area as is delineated in the sketch-map on page 6. Stretching from the three great sea lochs—Nevis, Hourn, and Duich—through Kintail to Glen Affric, it would include first-rate examples of all that is best in Highland scenery. The wild rocky hills known as the Rough Bounds of Knoydart, fine peaks like Sgùrr-na-Ciche, the Saddle, Ladhar Bheinn, and Scour Ouran, lovely freshwater lochs like Quoich, Affric, and Beneveian, and rivers and glen scenery like Glen Affric and Glen Cannich, would make up a wonderfully representative section of the country. It is traversed by the main through

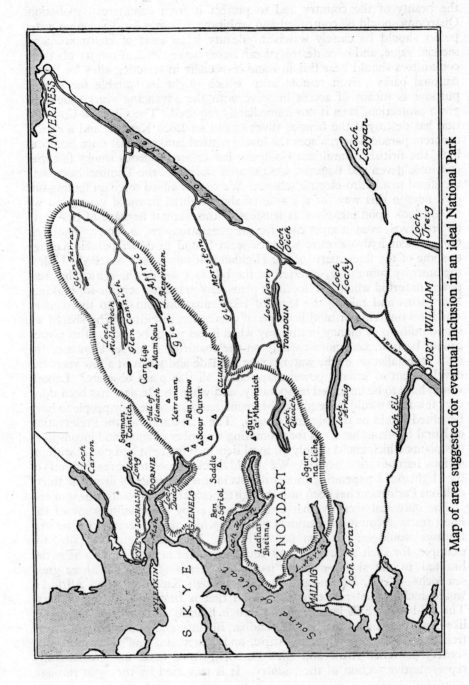

Map of area suggested for eventual inclusion in an ideal National Park

6 Sgùrr Fhuaran (Scour Ouran) from Loch Alsh

7 Loch Laidon (Rannoch Moor)

roads to Skye and the western isles, and communications could easily be improvised by sea in protected waters from Mallaig and Kyle of Lochalsh, both of which are served by railways.

The National Trust for Scotland has secured the nucleus of a magnificent national park in Glencoe and the adjoining property of Dalness, between it and Glen Etive. More recently it has acquired the Kintail Estate at the head of Loch Duich, including the fine group of hills known as the Five Sisters and Ben Attow. This adjoins a smaller property round the Falls of Glomach, the highest waterfall in Scotland, also owned by the Trust, and this would be a splendid beginning for the bigger plan outlined above.

It would be easy to pick out other suitable parts for preservation as national parks, such as the grand mountain region between Loch Torridon and Loch Maree, or special mountain groups like the hills of Arran or the Cuillin of Skye. These, however, are in less danger of spoliation as there is no water power available and the land is too barren for forestry.[1]

Another thing which will have a big effect on the scenery after the war is the resumption of its activities by the Forestry Commission. I have got into trouble by attacking this national institution, but I think my attitude has been misunderstood. I should be among the first to acknowledge the value of the work done by it and the prime necessity of replacing and extending the woodlands destroyed by the demands of war. The Commission has shown itself efficient and has done much splendid work, but its very efficiency has sometimes blinded its officials to considerations of amenity. A commercial plantation of conifers necessarily lacks the variety and beauty of a natural and less formal wood, but though we must have them in vast quantities my plea is for a little more consideration in their location. Special beauty-spots should be avoided, or planted where possible with broad-leaved trees, and where naturally sown forest exists it should be preserved as far as can

[1] Since the above was written, a report on proposed National Parks by the Scottish National Parks Survey Committee to the Secretary of State for Scotland has been published. Five areas are recommended as suitable for immediate attention and three others for subsequent consideration. The first five are: (1) Loch Lomond-Trossachs; (2) Glen Affric, Glen Cannich, Strath Farrar; (3) Ben Nevis, Glencoe, Black Mount; (4) Cairngorms; (5) Loch Torridon, Loch Maree, Little Loch Broom. Of these (1) is most accessible to the public, but Loch Katrine has already been seriously damaged, and it is to be hoped tnat the Loch Sloy hydro-electric scheme can be so carried out as to deface as little as possible the shores of Loch Lomond. (2) is included in the area suggested above in the text. It adjoins the fine Kintail property recently acquired by the National Trust. If only the boundary could be extended southwards across Glen Shiel to include the range of the Saddle, Loch Quoich, and the wild country of Knoydart with the great sea lochs—Duich, Hourn, and Nevis—as shown in our sketch-map, we should have a grand connected area of the very highest natural beauty preserved for all time. Knoydart is among the three reserve areas under the Survey, but if included in our inclusive scheme it would be much more important than Morar or Moidart. Loch Quoich needs prompt protection as it has more than once been threatened by the hydro-electric engineer. (3) includes Glencoe, already safe in the hands of the National Trust, and Ben Nevis and the Mamore Forest would be a grand addition to it. (4) The Cairngorms are popular with powerful walkers and are easily reached by the east coast route. The scenery is not so fine as that of the west coast, but the region includes the loftiest continuous ridges in Scotland. (5) includes the magnificent ranges of Ben Alligin, Beinn Eighe, Liathach, and An Teallach as well as Loch Maree. Where the natural woodlands along the shore of that loch have escaped the drastic treatment meted out by the Forestry Commission they should be religiously safeguarded.

be done, or at least a broad belt of it spaced along road or river or along the shores of a loch. If the conifer plantations could thus be kept in the background the blanketing effect of them on the hillsides would be less disastrous to the beauty of the landscape. Such special areas as we find in Glen Affric, whose beauty depends on the wild natural growth of the woods and heather should be preserved intact as national parks, and if elsewhere the Forestry people could be induced to act more in the spirit of the eighteenth century landlords, to whose planting the England we love owes so much of its beauty, they would earn the blessings of generations yet to come.

The main object of this book is to prove what a glorious holiday resort we have at our doors in these hills and islands of the west coast. Nowhere can purer air be found than on these exposed hills swept for ever by the Atlantic gales and cleansed by the showers of rain or snow which lend such a charm to the swiftly changing scene. I even venture to claim that under certain conditions the scenery of the western coast can be as beautiful as anything to be found the whole world over. We have no jagged rocks to rival those of the Dolomites and no gleaming glaciers to set against those of the Alps, but against this we have the sea. Everywhere the long arms of the sea penetrate far inland, and in whatever direction we go we are sure, sooner or later, to catch a glimpse of the salt water and taste the freshness of the salt sea-breeze. It is this wonderful mixture of mountain and sea which gives its unique charm to this enchanted region. The purple hills mirrored in the winding channels, the distant ranges and islands fading away into the blue distance, and the whole flecked by the changing shadows of the sunlit clouds, make up a picture that seems to be too delicate, too exquisitely lovely, to be real. On the best days the whole is bathed in an atmosphere of translucent colour that can be matched only among the isles of Greece. One must confess that it is not always thus. Bad weather, to put it mildly, is not unknown on the west coast, and even a spell of fine weather, if it comes with an east wind, is apt to produce a dull haze which blots out the distance and takes the colour out of the landscape. But when the right day does come, with the air washed clear by recent showers, the sky dappled with white broken cloud and the whole land and seascape sparkling in the spring sunshine, then, I say, the world has nothing better to offer, and a few days of this kind make up for weeks of waiting.

To enjoy the best that the west coast has to offer one must be prepared to leave the roads and tramp over rough ground and pathless hills, and to face the uncertainties of the weather; but no exceptional physical strength is necessary. Something may, no doubt, be seen from a motor-car, but the right use of the car is as a base of operations, to enable one to cover the duller portions of the road which separate the inn from the fairest beauty-spots, and enable one to arrive sufficiently fresh to tackle the steep slopes which may have to be surmounted before the best point of all can be reached.

In many ways the Highlands have preserved their wild character better than the more famous tourist regions of Europe. For instance, the great Alpine lakes, especially those on the Italian side, have little of the wild

8 Beinn Dorain—Winter

9 Loch Ard and Ben Lomond

natural shores that are one of the most attractive features of the Scottish lochs. Villas and gardens crowd along their margins, and it is not always easy to reach the edge of the water. Picturesque villages piled up on a rocky spur, or a church tower crowning a promontory, are prominent features of the scene, but the visitor comes away with a feeling that he has been studying art rather than nature. I have walked for miles along the Lake of Anneçy in search of a foreground for a picture, while the road, winding behind gardens or following the shore on an embankment, introduced unpleasing lines which prevented me from securing a satisfactory picture until I could find a slight eminence which commanded a bird's-eye view over the lake. In Scotland, however, there is a picture to be had every few yards, and in the sea-lochs the fall of the tide reveals piles of rocks and seaweed, which serve as an excellent foil to the beauties beyond.

People with only a casual acquaintance with the country often complain of the uncertainty of the weather, but surely the weather is one of the things one visits the Highlands to see! It is over a broad stretch of water backed by hills that the grandest effects of storm and shower, of towering cumulus or glowing sunset, can best be watched. For the photographer there is no more fascinating game than to lie in wait for the passing effects of storm and sunshine as the snow or hail showers sweep over the hills or across a loch, especially when the sun breaks through to light up the scene, and produce those contrasts of light and shade which give the most exciting opportunities for the camera. Best of all are the bright intervals between showers, or the clearing-up effects after rain. Very striking pictures, like that in (2), may be obtained under such conditions, when the piled-up masses of cloud are illumined from behind by the low afternoon sun, and their shadows are reflected in the water of the bay. I have elsewhere[1] described this sport of mountain photography, this hunting of Nature's striking effects, or patient waiting for the right moment, and many examples of the results so obtained will be found in the following pages.

Now this kind of brilliant changeable weather is most often met with in the spring, and this brings me to another point which I wish to emphasize, and that is, that from my point of view, that of the tramper and photographer, the spring is the best time to visit the Western Highlands. Apart from the fact that few impediments are placed in the way of the wanderer over the hills, even in the deer forests at a season when his presence can do no harm, the weather is usually finer in March, April, and May than later in the season, and even if unsettled is less likely to have long spells of hopeless rain than in August, when many people crowd the hotels. The April-shower type of weather is the most beautiful of all, and if the peaks of the higher hills are picked out with a covering of snow this adds a brilliance to the landscape more valuable—to the photographer, at any rate—than even the more gorgeous colouring of autumn. A fresh fall of snow lit up by bright sunshine, with white clouds floating overhead, as in the illustration in (3), of Cul Mòr, as seen from Canisp, adds a brilliance to the landscape which

---

[1] *The Art and Sport of Alpine Photography* (Witherby, 1927).

is of dazzling beauty, especially when the stately mountain outlines are backed by the distant glimmer of the sea.

The snow, too, which remains on the higher peaks until quite late in the spring, and even lasts through the summer in some of the cracks of the northern precipices of Ben Nevis and some other big mountains, is a great help to the photographer in more than one way. Two photographs taken from Sgùman Còinntich, a hill 2,881 feet high, over Killilan on the Ross-shire Loch Long, will serve to illustrate two ways in which it is helpful. To begin with, one of the difficulties which the camera has to contend with is that the foreground usually requires a longer exposure than the distant view, but if that foreground is sprinkled with white snow that trouble disappears. Again a distant mountain, which might otherwise be too faintly seen to be effective, if snow-clad, and especially if lit up by the sun, is brought out clearly and brightens up the picture in a way which could be done by no other means. Thus, in (4), Sgùrr-nan-Ceathreamhnan (Kerranan) stands up clearly, with every ridge picked out by the white covering, which also gives it a dignity as it towers over the less lofty black or merely dappled ranges.

Plate 5 also illustrates the remarks made a page or two back about the wonderful mixture of sea and land in this favoured district. In the middle distance on the left is Loch Alsh, backed by the hills of Skye, the main group of which rise beyond the more open arm of the sea on the farther side of the narrows at Kyle. Loch Duich is hidden by the nearer hills on the extreme left of the picture, while the head of Loch Long appears at our feet on the right. This picture gives an excellent idea of the intricate coastline, with its winding channels and long arms of the sea running far inland among the rugged hills.

How the spring snow adds to the majesty of the higher peaks may be shown by a view looking up towards Scour Ouran (Sgùrr Fhuaran, 3,505 feet), at the head of Loch Duich, from the shores of Loch Alsh (6). When this photograph was taken there had been a fresh sprinkle of snow on the tops, and when a gleam of sunshine caught this sharp and stately peak it stood out like an Alpine giant, especially when the shades of evening were drawing in, or the nearer scene was subdued under a heavy cloud.

Spring then is the time for the walker or the photographer to visit the Highlands. He will find room in the inns and cheaper prices, he will be free to wander over the hills without let or hindrance, he will find the scenery at its best, and his chances of good weather better than at any other time. The gorse will begin to blaze its trail of gold and the primroses will deck the banks and cliffs. In the later spring the flowers may be even better, and the young leaves of the birches add fresh beauty to the May sunshine, but the snow will have begun to melt, except in specially late seasons, and as summer approaches the green of the bracken with that of the trees introduces a uniformity of colour which perhaps lacks the charm of the richer hues of autumn or the brilliance of the spring snow.

But if spring is my favourite season in the Highlands I would be the last to deny the charms of the rest of the year. The Gulf Stream brings an equable climate, with less violent contrasts between summer and winter than in the south, though the short days of winter are more of a drawback. But the perfect day may come in July or September as well as in April, and those who cannot take a holiday in the spring will be able to drink their fill of beauty whenever they visit this enchanted coast. It is useless to dogmatize about west coast weather: anything may happen at any time. Ben Nevis may be white with snow in August, and in 1932 February was described by the inhabitants as a whole month of summer weather without a shower. The balmy air of June may be more comfortable than the cold blasts of April, but the midges may be a plague in the heather. The point, however, which I wish to make is that the best chance of interesting weather and of enjoying the supreme beauties of the West Highlands is to be found fairly early in the year.

I have sometimes been asked what I considered to be the most beautiful view in Scotland. This is an impossible question to answer, and I think the best response is that it all depends on the weather! The most glorious views lose much of their charm on a hazy day, while quite ordinary landscapes acquire a wonderful beauty in really favourable conditions. For instance, if there is a dull tract of bog and moorland in the Highlands it is to be found in the vast expanse of Rannoch Moor, whose monotony is relieved only by the distant outlines of the mountain ranges which surround it. Loch Laidon is a dull sheet of water with low-lying banks and little to give character to the view except the distant hills, which are set too far from the shores to be really effective. But even here (7) on a bright April day, with sunlit clouds casting shadows over the water, it is quite possible to find a picture of infinite beauty if a slightly more interesting bit of bank can be selected, with rocks and sand glistening in the sunshine to give interest. It is true that certain scenes stand out in the memory as some of the supreme visions of Highland beauty, but most of these were brief glimpses under fleeting conditions, and a second visit to the same spot might be fraught with disappointment. Such a view was that from one of the lesser hills of Arran, to be described later in our last chapter (pp. 105 and 106), and now a sunset from Morar or Ballachulish (37, 38, 42, 104 to 107), now a view of the bare rocks surrounding Loch Scavaig, with a blue and green sea glistening in the sunshine and a dark storm hanging over the gloomy recesses of Loch Coruisk and the beetling crags of the Cuillin (236), now a stretch of sea and island from some point of vantage on the coast, call up memories of unforgettable beauty, but where all are so glorious it is difficult to award the palm to any one. Let us be thankful for the ever-changing vagaries of the west coast weather which are always presenting us with this superb pageant of beauty, passing from glory to glory in successive scenes never quite the same, but always lovely!

Even winter has its charms if a spell of fine weather can be caught. The days are short, but snow effects are often of great beauty. Bold spirits of the Scottish Mountaineering Club have been in the habit of organizing a new year meet in some of the more accessible regions, and though I have not myself ventured among the hills at that inhospitable season I am able to insert a photograph taken by my brother on an occasion when the meet took place at Crianlarich and was favoured with exceptionally fine weather (8). Snow is certainly a good friend to the photographer, but it may be doubted whether an all-over covering of it does not detract from the dignity of the higher peaks, which gain immensely in apparent height when only their upper portion is picked out in snow.

A few words may not be out of place here on the *sport* of mountain photography.[1] I have used the word designedly, as to make good pictures of this class of landscape much the same qualities are required as are needed to make a good sportsman in the usual meaning of the word. Patience, waiting for the right effect, readiness to seize the opportunity when it comes, quickness in appreciating the necessary conditions of composition and lighting to be most effective; all those are just as much wanted to direct the camera as the gun.

But in other ways the serious photographer[2] comes out still better in the comparison. Not only is his art comparatively cheap, but it is constructive, not destructive. The grouse shooter, when he has eaten his bird, has nothing to show for his prowess beyond an empty memory of the number of brace he has brought down, but the photographer who has chased his effect over the hills with success has a pictorial record that can give him pleasure for the rest of his days—or, at any rate, until he has produced a better.

Except painting there is perhaps no better æsthetic training for the eye than the art of the camera, and, to my mind, a good photograph is more satisfactory than any painting, save that of a real master of the craft.

The contemplation and appreciation of the beauty of nature, especially in its grandest manifestations, when sea and mountain forms are so inextricably mixed as on the west coast of Scotland, are a refining and ennobling experience; and an art that brings us into closer touch with such scenes not only brings joy and peace to our hearts, but is also one of the best forms of education for our souls.

To search out the best viewpoint, to be there at the right moment when weather and lighting conditions are perfect, is a fascinating pursuit, and no easy one; but nature is full of delightful surprises, and frequently our most successful picture is not of the view we have tramped miles to secure, but of some unexpected beauty, suddenly revealed in all its glory, which has burst upon us on our way.

For this reason it is one of the secrets of success in this class of work always to have the camera ready, on every expedition, for the fickle climate of the west coast is full of surprises, and only those who are ready to seize the opportunity when it comes will reap the reward.

It is therefore better to rely on small and light apparatus which can be carried easily, and I recommend the popular quarter-plate camera (4¼ in. by

[1] I have elaborated this subject in my book on *The Art and Sport of Alpine Photography*.

[2] I do not, of course, take too seriously the mere snap-shotter, who lets fly at anything, and sends his films to a professional to be developed. He may meet with an occasional success, half by accident, but experience and taste are required to produce something more.

$3\frac{1}{4}$ in.) as the most suitable. Enlargements can be made to any reasonable size, and if glass plates are used, the burden of carrying larger sizes becomes a weariness to the flesh.

Lenses should not be of too short a focal length or there will be a tendency to dwarf the mountains, but if a long-focus lens be adopted there will be difficulty in dealing with the foreground. For general purposes a lens of $5\frac{1}{2}$ in. to 6 in. focus will be found most convenient for a quarter-plate camera, and though a good lens is a luxury, a very expensive one is not altogether indispensable for this class of work.

Great care is necessary in selecting a suitable foreground, as this is one of the most essential elements in producing a good composition. Something is always wanted to give the right balance, and throw the distance into the proper perspective, and this is one of the first problems that a beginner in this class of work must study.

In making a picture, too, it should be remembered that photography, as the name implies, is the art of delineating objects by means of light and shadow. The best results will not always be those which appeal to the painter in colour, for colour-photography has not yet reached the stage when it can give a really satisfactory reproduction of the more delicate gradations of the colours of nature.

The most effective shading and light contrasts are to be found in the clouds, and nowhere are clouds to be seen in greater glory than among the mountains, or over the sea. It is, therefore, in the kind of weather that we associate with April showers that the photographer of broad landscapes of the kind illustrated in this book will find his best inspiration.

That is one reason why, as already stated above, I claim that the early spring is the best season for the Highlands. A long period of set-fair weather, with an easterly wind, is apt to produce a haze which takes all the life and beauty out of the landscape, and though suitable for mountain ascents it will not give the photographer much opportunity except for small subjects or detailed work.

Ingenious people sometimes attempt to produce striking effects by combining clouds from one picture with a landscape from another. Such productions, however, will seldom satisfy the eye of a trained artist, or keen observer of nature, in a big landscape. Here the sky should be an essential part of the picture, and it is almost impossible to get all the shadows and reflections right in a composite picture, especially where water is a feature. I have therefore avoided all such devices in the pictures here reproduced,[1] and for the kind of subject here treated I have kept to the old-fashioned straight photograph as the only one giving satisfactory results for the purpose set before me. There are many methods adopted by show photographers for suppression of unnecessary detail, or for making their productions look like etchings or paintings, but these usually mean sacrificing the very elements in which the camera excels in a hopeless attempt to compete with results much better attained through another medium.

[1] With one insignificant exception, which I leave to the reader's eye to discover.

Those who intend taking a holiday in the Highlands on the lines suggested in this book must adopt one of two plans. The young and active may put a rucksack on their backs and tramp from place to place through the valleys or over the hills as circumstances or weather conditions tempt them, sleeping each night in some fresh place, and prepared, if necessary, even to face a night out under a rock. They are able thus to keep farther from the beaten track, and to reach spots which are inaccessible to those who have to get back to one of the sparsely scattered inns forming their base of operations.

Personally, however—and I think most men who have reached middle age will agree with me—I prefer the second alternative of fixing upon some one centre from which to explore the surrounding country, and then, if the holiday is long enough, moving on to another. This scheme allows a reasonable quantity of baggage, and changes of clothes, especially of boots—that greatest comfort of all!

Weight-carrying comes easily to some, but I must confess that I find the pleasure of a long walk much interfered with by a heavy burden on my back, and the photographic apparatus, a light mackintosh and the lunch, are quite as much as I care to carry.

The walks and explorations described in these pages have been made on this plan, and can, therefore, be repeated in reasonable comfort by any good walker who does not mind a rough tramp, or pine for unnecessary luxuries.

There are many varied types of scenery in the Highlands, and the object of this book is to try to give a record of some of the leading types rather than to provide a guide-book.

The chief division is between east and west from an artistic point of view; though geographically the Grampians or the Caledonian Canal might seem more obvious lines of demarcation. There is of course no fixed point at which one can say that east gives place to west, but there can be no doubt that the climate seems to change somewhere near the watershed.

It is often fine on one side when it is wet on the other, and the western valleys enjoy a much milder winter than the east coast. On the other hand the east is much drier than the west, and, though weather can never be depended on among mountains, there is more chance of fine settled days than in the west. In spite of this, however, there is a wonderful charm about the west country that more than makes up for this disadvantage. The very changeableness of the weather adds interest to the landscape, with fresh effects every hour, and new beauties revealed with every change of lighting or shifting of shadow.

I have no wish to belittle the loveliness of the wooded glens of Tay or Tummel,[1] or the grim solitudes of the Cairngorms, but there can be no question that the scenery of the west is finer. The long arms of the sea running for miles inland, the fringe of islands, the abrupt crags of the mountains, all give a diversity to the scene which can be found nowhere else. Everything is more compact, and the huge tracts of bog or dull moorland

[1] Serious damage has been done to the scenery of the Tummel by a hydro-electric installation.

Page 14

that separate the beauty-spots of the centre and east are much less evident or absent altogether.

The traveller by the Highland Railway between Perth and Inverness will realize my meaning. After leaving the woods at Blair Atholl, there is little of interest in the rounded and shapeless hills, or dreary uplands of Drummochter, until he gets down again to Kingussie or Aviemore. Here and there a glimpse of a lake gleaming like silver among the encompassing hills adds a touch of beauty to the scene, but for the most part I am quite content to leave these dreary wastes to the deer stalker and sportsman, if only he would allow better access to the glorious country beyond.

It is curious how much more room the eastern mountains seem to take up than the western. The result is that though higher than anything except Ben Nevis they do not look their height, and are far less impressive than the smaller but more abrupt ranges of Ross or Skye, or the isolated hills of Sutherland. It means a whole day's tramp to reach the foot of the Cairngorms, and to explore their tops and innermost recesses requires an expenditure of energy that makes the expedition an athletic feat rather than a pleasant ramble, and so puts them outside the scope of the present volume.

It is not mere altitude that makes a mountain impressive but comparative altitude, and the western hills preserve a much more satisfactory proportion between height and area. Then, too, it must be remembered that most of them rise straight up from sea-level, whereas the Cairngorms can only be seen from a wide valley itself 700 to 1,000 feet above the level of the sea.

Travellers from Inverness spend half a day in the train without losing sight of Ben Wyvis, a dull flat-topped lump of a hill that takes up as much room on the map as the whole many-peaked range of the Cuillin Hills in Skye. It is, therefore, with the more varied scenery of the west, its shapely hills and winding lochs, and above all that marvellous mixture of mountain, sea and sky that give it its peculiar fascination, that I propose to deal in this volume.

It remains to make the usual apology for my attitude towards the Gaelic spelling of the names. It is a pity that so many grand mountains should have been afflicted with such appalling names, given an even more forbidding appearance by the elaborate, pedantic methods adopted in the orthodox spelling.

It is difficult to feel the same intimate affection for a mountain whose name we cannot pronounce as we can feel for Scafell or Snowdon. The Gaelic language seems never to have been meant to be written down. It abounds in sounds that no tongue not brought up to it can produce; its genders are chaotic, and its inflexions affect the beginning or middle of the word rather than the end, making the ordinary type of dictionary almost useless.

It is claimed that the orthodox spelling is phonetic, but this end is only attained by an elaborate system of giving new sounds to letters, or to combinations of letters, which alter or cancel one another, and make the words so long and forbidding in appearance that they rouse the same sort of repulsion in the mind of a stranger that the old-fashioned art student feels on visiting an exhibition of Cubist pictures.

The names themselves are also very unsatisfactory. The ordnance surveyors seem to have twisted them about in a vain attempt to get some non-existent meaning into them, and where no native name existed they seem to have taken long descriptions, translated them into the best Gaelic they could manage, and to have used the sentence as a name.

If, on being questioned as to what he called a certain hill, the peasant replied that he usually described it as the red hill behind the son of So-and-so's cottage, the 'red hill behind the son of So-and-so's cottage' translated into Gaelic becomes the name the wretched hill has to go by ever after. Fortunately, about a quarter of all the mountains in Scotland are called the 'Red Mountain', and when one has learnt that DEARG is pronounced JERRUG one has the key to a very large proportion of the names.

Under these circumstances I have been tempted, whenever an anglicized form of a name has been at all widely recognized, to use this instead of frightening my English readers with its correct equivalent. But where these do not exist I have usually been forced to use the form adopted by the ordnance maps. The solution is not perfect, but seems best under the circumstances, and if I make no pretensions to be an authority in the matter I hope the purists will have the greater mercy.

As in the earlier book, I have tried to bring into close alliance the text and the illustrations. In a book of this kind I have no use for the method of writing the text first and then going and buying a few photographs at haphazard and inserting them in the volume to please the publisher and make it look more worth the price charged. I feel that as the days of eloquence, even in politics, are passing, long and flowery descriptions of scenery will convey far less to the average reader than even a moderately good photograph. The appeal to the eye, therefore, has been my main object, and in the accompanying text I have endeavoured to answer the questions which would occur to the reader turning over the picture pages. I have pointed out salient features, describing the conditions under which the photographs were taken; I have shown how to reach the places illustrated, and tried to fill in some of the features which are beyond the power of the camera to reproduce. The hunt after these pictures in fair weather and foul, over moor and bog and crag, beside stream or loch or sea, has been a source of endless pleasure to me. May they also help to induce others to follow in my footsteps and do something to enhance the fame of this favoured region, and bring home to the minds of an ever-widening circle the supreme beauty of this national heritage!

10 Head of Loch Etive

11 Ben Cruachan from Loch Etive

12　Loch Etive

13 Loch Long and the Cobbler

14 Jura from Kilmory

15 Ben More from Crianlarich

17 Loch Lomond

18 Ben Lomond

19 Loch Fyne

20 Jura from near Tayvallich

21 Mull from Seil

22 Loch Awe and Cruachan

23 Loch Awe looking towards Dalmally

24 Ben More and Stobinian

25 Cruach Ardrain

26 Ben Lui

27 Ben More, etc. from Beinn Chuirn

28 Loch Tay

29 Loch Rannoch and Schiehallion

30 Ben Cruachan, main peak

31 Loch Etive and Ben Nevis from Cruachan

E

32 Cruachan, Taynuilt Peak

33   Beinn a'Bheithir (Ben Vair) from Ballachulish

34 Garbh-bheinn from Kentallen

35 Garbh-bheinn from Ballachulish

36 Ballachulish Ferry—a Passing Shower

37 Sunset from Ballachulish

38 Sunset from Ballachulish

THIS CHAPTER WILL DEAL WITH places south of the Caledonian Canal, with the exception of the Glencoe and Ben Nevis regions, which deserve a chapter to themselves. As most of the well-known tourist resorts are to be found in this part of the country I propose to treat it in a rather summary fashion in order to leave room for a more detailed description of the lesser-known regions farther north.

One of the best of the easily accessible centres from which to explore the beauties of the Southern Highlands may be found at Arrochar, on the West Highland Railway. It is situated at the head of Loch Long, just at the narrow isthmus separating this salt-water loch from Loch Lomond. From this strategic point, expeditions may be made not only along the shores of both lochs, but to the surrounding hills, and they can be extended at will by making use of the railway.

Loch Long is long and narrow, and gradually increases in interest as the head is approached, though the ugly sheds recently erected by the pier, in connection with the submarine station not far from Arrochar, are a blot on the landscape.

The chief feature of Loch Long is the mountain usually known as the Cobbler (13), whose extraordinary outline is the most remarkable thing of its kind in the Southern Highlands. The actual summit is a tower, which presents something of a problem to the inexperienced rock-climber, but the main platform from which it rises is easily reached from the back in spite of the formidable appearance of the eastern face of the mountain.

For those who possess a car there is a fine drive to be made from Arrochar through Glen Croe to Loch Fyne (19) and Inverary, and thence to Ardrishaig and Tarbert in the Mull of Kintyre. The drive to Campbeltown and right round this long peninsula has fine views over the sea in both directions, to the west towards the fine outline of the Paps of Jura (14), and to the east over the bold hills of Arran. From Ardrishaig, too, the road past the Crinan Canal to Loch Melfort and Oban, with its views across the Firth of Lorne to Jura and Mull (20, 21), or that along Loch Awe to Dalmally, with its views of Cruachan across the loch, seen from the park-like country of its south-eastern shores, makes a very pleasant round (22, 23).

Loch Lomond is so well known that it needs no description here. The finest part is the narrow northern half, where the hills descend in steep crags into the water, but the wider southern portion, though the shores are comparatively tame, can look grand in stormy weather, with black clouds driving

E*

across the heavens, their dark and ragged edges rendered all the more gloomy by a few stray rays of watery sunshine from the realms beyond, while the sullen waters of the lake are lashed by the gale into angry little wavelets breaking on the stony shore (17).

From the greater part of the loch the cone of Ben Lomond is a striking feature (18), but the finest mountain outline is that seen across the loch from Inversnaid, the pier at which tourists land for the coach bound for the Trossachs. Lovers of a quiet life will do well to let the crowd hurry on in the coach and themselves linger awhile in this beautiful spot before walking on to poor mutilated Loch Katrine. The hills on the farther shore rise to over 3,000 feet in height, and form a noble group, which looks especially impressive when the weather is clearing up after rain, and low clouds are rolling round the flanks of the mountains, adding enormously to their apparent size (16).

There is a pleasant drive from the Trossachs over the shoulder of Ben Venue to Aberfoyle and Loch Ard. From the top of the pass a pretty glimpse may be had of wooded Loch Drunkie in a hollow far below, and there is a wide view of the Lowlands from this Highland rampart. Loch Ard presents a very different picture from the wild scene described in Scott's *Rob Roy*, for villas and country houses spread half-way along its shores, but the farther end is still more or less untouched, and Ben Lomond stands up well at the head. Our photograph (9) was taken when a north-west gale was lashing these inland waters into a miniature copy of the sea and dotting the whole surface of the loch with foam.

Crianlarich, where the West Highland and Callander and Oban railways intersect, is another excellent centre. It is also a good place at which those who dislike night travelling used to break their journey, as there was a good day train to London, reaching Euston in time for bed, though there was still no corresponding service in the other direction, Stirling and Perth being the best halting-places on the way to the north-west from London.

Crianlarich is situated in a wide upland valley, 500 or 600 feet above the sea, of a rather desolate and severe character, except where the river widens out into little lakes. It is surrounded by lofty and imposing mountains, of which the twin peaks of Ben More (3,843 feet) and Stobinian (Am Binnein, 3,827 feet) are the highest (24). When deep in snow, as the present writer saw them in the snowy spring of 1922, they look very fine, especially when seen from a few miles away on either side of the village, far enough off to get a profile view of the range with the two great pyramids in their proper proportion.

From Crianlarich itself Ben More alone is visible (15), but it towers up grandly over the valley. The next mountain to the westward, Cruach Ardrain (3,428 feet), is a fine object (25), but perhaps the finest view of all is obtained when approaching Tyndrum, the next station on the railway, where there is also an hotel, which makes a good stopping-place. Here a long, straight valley branches off with the magnificent form of Ben Lui (Laoigh, 3,708 feet) at its head. Covered with snow, as it was in 1922 when the photograph reproduced in (26) was taken, this mountain presented quite an Alpine appearance. But, as we were in bad training at the beginning of a holiday, we hesitated to attack such a formidable peak, and were tempted to climb instead a lower height on the other side of the valley called Beinn Chuirn (2,878 feet), partly because the lower slopes were less buried in snow, and partly because we felt that, under such conditions, the view of Ben Lui would be finer than the view from Ben Lui. Our expectations were more than justified, as not only did Ben Lui look magnificent all the time, but a wonderful panorama was spread out before us in every other direction as well. To the west Cruachan raised its double peak; farther north a sea of mountains faded away in the direction of Ben Nevis, while nearer at hand Ben More, Stobinian, and Cruach Ardrain rose proudly over the intervening ridges, gleaming in their snowy mantle, and looking so vast through a slight haze that one could almost imagine them some great Himalayan range instead of the modest hills of our own familiar land (27).

By the help of the railways many other good expeditions can be made from Crianlarich. The upper end of Loch Lomond, Loch Tulla, and Loch Tay can all be reached easily. We illustrate Loch Tay (28) from the Kenmore end: one of the few photographs in this book not taken in the spring but on one of those showery days of early autumn that recall the memory of April showers, when the brilliance of the sunshine is set off by the heavy but broken clouds, and the strong breeze lashes the surface of the loch into miniature copies of Atlantic rollers that dance and sparkle in the glorious light.

Travellers by the West Highland Railway will remember the famous sugar-loaf view of Schiehallion (3,547 feet) across Rannoch Moor. It is well worth while to cross the moor to the shores of Loch Rannoch in order to admire this shapely pyramid rising in isolated splendour over the loch, and commanding all the country around. It is especially effective after a fresh fall of snow (29).

Ben Cruachan (3,689 feet) has the reputation of being the finest mountain in the Southern Highlands, and, on the whole, this reputation is justified. It is a collection of seven or eight peaks, of which two are considerably higher than the others, and connected by a rocky ridge or saddle. Like Ben Nevis it is a shy mountain, for it is difficult to get a good general view of it except from a considerable distance, and only those who penetrate its innermost recesses can appreciate its real grandeur.

Ben Cruachan is best visited from Taynuilt, though Dalmally and the Loch Awe Hotel are also good starting-places. As they are all joined by the railway it does not much matter where the night is spent, but we voted for Taynuilt, as Loch Etive is more beautiful than Loch Awe.

Nobody visiting this region should omit to wander, at any rate for some distance, along the shores of Loch Etive. Long and narrow, it winds among the hills like a vast river, and the varied outlines of the surrounding mountains, backed, in the spring in any case, by the snow-capped heights over Glencoe, make up a never-to-be-forgotten picture, especially on a glorious spring day with sunlit clouds drifting over the blue of the sky, and dappling the hillsides with their fleeting shadows (12).

Loch Etive can also be approached by a little road which runs south from the Glencoe road near Kingshouse; it enables the upper part of the loch to be seen which is rather inaccessible from the south. Ben Starav (3,541 feet) is a fine feature, and farther off Cruachan presents its steepest and most formidable face (10, 11).

Our first attempt on Cruachan was made on a bright but unsettled morning, and we chose the Dalmally route as likely to give us a pleasant high-level walk to the summit. The ascent to the end of the ridge is quite a simple matter, but just after we had accomplished all the hard work, and were looking forward to the fine ridge walk, we were suddenly enveloped in a sharp little snowstorm, which proved the forerunner of a series. We pushed on, however, in the intervals, enjoying the grand cloud effects as furious little squalls of snow and hail chased one another over the landscape, the clouds sometimes forming a solid-looking arch from one peak to the next, and sometimes obliterating everything from our view.

As we reached the foot of the final peak the snow began in good earnest, and looked like settling down for the rest of the day. Such conditions made it necessary to abandon the rest of the expedition and beat a retreat towards a less inhospitable region lower down. We accordingly made our way down into a deep corrie at our feet, and, after sliding and slipping down the steep snow-covered slopes, emerged from the snowcloud to find that we had not lost our sense of direction, but were in a valley leading straight down to the road beside the shores of Loch Awe.

Our next attempt was made under very different conditions. The morning was a perfect one, and, wishing to run no risks of a change, we made straight for the nearer summit, which we reached with little trouble, and no difficulties beyond one or two steep pitches.

The view from the second, or Taynuilt peak, which is only 70 or 80 feet lower than the main summit, is much the finest, as it juts out towards Loch Etive in such a way as to command that beautiful arm of the sea from end to end, while the spurs of the main peak cut off the dreary moorland which forms the middle distance in the view from the highest summit. The main peak itself, too, is a fine object, especially when glittering with snow from top to bottom, as it was on that beautiful May day. Ben More and Ben Lui were peeping over its shoulder, their white tops glistening in the sunshine (30).

The weather was absolutely perfect from a photographer's point of view: the air was so clear that the Isle of Rum, though sixty miles away, could be distinctly seen in a small negative when developed, and even some of the islands of the Outer Hebrides could be made out. Glorious clouds were floating in the blue, with brilliant sunshine pouring through the spaces between them, lighting up their upper surfaces and casting blue-black shadows on their flanks.

Water adds enormously to the variety and beauty of a mountain landscape, and the view of Loch Etive, threading its way through the encircling hills till it ended beneath the splendid Glencoe peaks, made an absolutely perfect picture (31) on this wonderful day. Towering above even the Glencoe heights the familiar bluff outline of Ben Nevis asserted its supremacy, while farther away still ridge beyond ridge melted away into the distance. The nearer rocks were all covered with snow feathers three or four inches long, apparently formed by a wet mist driven against them by a freezing wind, and produced a very picturesque effect.

The Taynuilt peak (32) is not quite so fine as the other, but it makes a good foreground for the distant view of sea and mountain melting away into the west.

The ridge between the two peaks proved far less exacting than the guide-book descriptions had led us to expect, but perhaps the snow filling up some of the cracks between the big boulders made progress easier than it would have been later in the year.

After we had spent an hour or so drinking in the marvellous view, a curious gloom seemed to crawl up from the south, gradually swallowing up the distance and taking all the colour from the sparkling blue atmosphere; so we turned our steps homeward in order to reach our base of operations before we could be caught by the rain which the untoward change in the sky predicted. Just as we had packed up ready to descend a great golden eagle came sailing over the crags at our feet, and if the camera had been ready for action we might have added a new and unusual type of picture to this collection.

III

Ballachulish is a good headquarters, as it can be reached by road or rail, and in the summer also by steamboat. The branch line from Connell Ferry links it to Oban or to the railway to the south via Callander and Stirling. By getting up before breakfast it was, before the War, even possible to reach London without having to face the discomfort of a night journey. By the way, why is it that it is always made easier to reach London from Scotland than the reverse? I hate travelling by night, as I am a light sleeper, and if I have to break the journey going north I cannot get beyond Callander in one day, whereas on the return journey there is a day train from Oban. It is the same on the other line: it is not possible to go beyond Perth, or at most Blair-Atholl, in the day, but going south there is a good train from Inverness to London. Is this one reason why so many Scotsmen come to London to manage our affairs for us, and, in spite of their pride in and affection for their own country, seem to prefer the fleshpots of the south to the rugged simplicity of their northern fastnesses?

But to return to Ballachulish. The hotels are beautifully situated, with glorious views across Loch Linnhe, and a ferry plies between them across the narrow entrance to Loch Leven. The lofty ridges of Ben Vair (Beinn a'Bheithir) tower up at the back, and the peaks seen at the head of the corries between the great buttresses enclosing them present quite an Alpine appearance after a fall of snow (33). There is a beautiful road beside the water to Kentallen, and on to Oban. For part of the way the railway shuts off the shore, though every here and there the photographer is tempted to do a little trespass across the line to secure a picture of the fine range of hills on the other side of the loch (34). The finest of these is Garbh-bheinn (2,903 feet), whose grand crags present a formidable appearance even at this distance, and the deep depression of Glen Tarbert, which provides a way through to Loch Sunart, helps to give a varied and broken skyline. Farther to the north is another deep hollow, Glen Gour, though this is backed by a range of shapely hills instead of piercing right through the tangled range of mountains.

On the occasion of one of my visits to Ballachulish I enjoyed a week-end of wild spring weather. High winds and snow made any attempt on Ben Vair out of the question, but though we were confined to the hotel for long hours together by hopeless rain there were at times bright intervals in which we could sally forth with mackintosh and camera to watch the beautiful effects over the water when the sun struggled through between the showers, or lit up the peaks opposite gleaming in their brilliant mantle of fresh-fallen snow (35). Ballachulish is peculiarly well situated for watching the weather, as the loch is broad enough to give a wide and extensive panorama across the water, but not so wide as to dwarf the hills altogether, while breaks in the clouds are more frequent over a wide space than among densely packed peaks. Plate 36 is an attempt to catch a passing snow-shower over the ferry. Garbh-bheinn is just seen like a ghost through the last flakes of snow trailing behind the storm, while bright sunshine is lighting up the clouds and hills on the right over Glen Gour. Ballachulish is also an excellent spot from which to watch the sunset, as it faces west, and the shapely hills across the water are not too near to shut out all but the latest phase of the most glorious pageant of the heavens. Three stormy sunsets are given here, with the sun going down behind Garbh-bheinn and leaving a trail of light across the water (37, 38, 42). The camera cannot reproduce the full glory of colours, but where the effect aimed at is more one of light and shade than of colour, it can make a tolerably good attempt to record the most impressive scene of Nature's repertoire.

Crossing the ferry one wild evening, we had a splendid effect from the beach half-way to Onich (43). A heavy storm-cloud hung low over Garbh-bheinn, and from behind its dark folds the sun shot down rays of light which were reflected in the foaming waves that the gale had lashed up into fury even in these narrow waters.

Ballachulish possesses another advantage. A few minutes' walk along the east-bound road brings one round a corner, and a new view opens up over Loch Leven backed by the splendid peaks over Glencoe. There is thus an eastward as well as a westward view across the water and weather effects can be studied over loftier and nearer peaks as well as over the more distant ranges beyond Loch Linnhe. The sugar-loaf peak, Sgòr-na-Ciche, or Pap of Glencoe (2,430 feet), is a striking feature of the view (44), and is backed by the higher mass of Aonach Eagach (3,168 feet), whose serrated ridges form the northern wall of the narrow Pass of Glencoe. To the left of this group runs the upper reach of Loch Leven, while the depression on the right is that of the famous pass. Our stormy week-end provided some striking snow-shower effects in this direction as well as in the other, and a couple of them are reproduced (44, 45). It is extraordinary what a variety of effect can be obtained in pictures taken from the same spot under different weather conditions. The two given here were taken in intervals between violent showers of hail or snow, and the contrasts of light and shade, the glimpses of mysterious crags revealed in a momentary parting of the driving vapours, the long sweep of the snow-blizzards, formed a fascinating and magnificent spectacle, and provided numerous opportunities for the camera.

While looking at this view I am tempted to refer to an unnecessary blot on the landscape, though it does not show up in our pictures. The hideous mess caused by the great slate quarries is regrettable, but may have some economic justification; the architect, however, who roofed the large mansion at the foot of the Pap of Glencoe with bright red tiles has introduced an inharmonious note into the landscape. It is an axiom among all town and country planners that local and sympathetic materials should be used in buildings, especially in such a prominent position.[1]

The ascent of Ben Vair presents no difficulties, and is well worth making as it occupies a prominent position somewhat isolated from its neighbours and commanding a wide prospect over sea and land. Bidean-nam-Bian towers up above Glencoe (39), and Ben Nevis and the Mamore Forest heights rise above the ridges over Loch Leven, usually snow-capped in the spring (40). There are two peaks joined by an interesting but easy saddle.

Ballachulish has one disadvantage as a base of operations for the mountain rambler. For all ascents except that of Ben Vair he has to follow the four miles of road to Coe Bridge, more than half of it through a mining village or the hideous debris of the immense slate quarries, and from Coe Bridge it is a tramp of two or three miles more to the heart of Glencoe. A motor-car would therefore be a great assistance in most of his expeditions, unless he prefers to secure more homely and primitive accommodation in the little inn at Clachaig, which is admirably placed as a centre from which to explore the fine hills which shut in the pass, or the new hotel recently opened where the great new road debouches on the sea. The highest of the Glencoe mountains is Bidean-nam-Bian (3,766 feet), the crowning height of Argyll, and a good general view of it can be obtained from the north shore of Loch Leven (41). The summit is half hidden behind the great shoulder called An-t-Sron, but the second peak, Stob-Coire-nan-Lochan, has a sharp point and stands out well to the left above a corrie filled with snow in springtime. When our picture was taken there were some of those curious flattened oval clouds about, which look like hats forming over the peaks, and seem to indicate unsettled weather.

A nearer view is obtainable from the lower part of the glen above Coe Bridge (46). Here the valley is well wooded, and the smiling landscape backed by finely shaped mountains is a great contrast to the savage grandeur of the upper glen. I do not propose to wax sentimental over the grim story of the famous Massacre of 1692, which took place near the mouth of the river, and far from the wilder parts of the glen which the imagination pictures as a suitable setting for such a scene. Although King William cannot be exonerated from all share in the blame, this was really one of the series of horrible acts of brutality and treachery which have so often stained the annals of Scottish history. It is wonderful how proud the Scot is of his ancestry; when one remembers the way in which those barbarous ancestors carried on one would have thought that the less said about them the better !

Much controversy has been roused over the new road through Glencoe, and Dr. E. A. Baker has referred to it as 'the new massacre of Glencoe'. It stands to reason that a modern speedway cannot be driven through a wild

[1] Since the above was written the red tiles have been removed, and the result has been an immense improvement.

39 Bidean-nam-Bian from Ben Vair

40 Loch Leven from Ben Vair

41 Glencoe from Loch Leven

42   Sunset from Ballachulish

43 A Stormy Evening—North Ballachulish

44 Loch Leven—Wild Weather

45 Loch Leven—Snow Showers

46 Lower Glencoe

47 Loch Achtriochtan

48 Glencoe

F

49 Ben Nevis and Mamore Forest from ridge above Glencoe

50 Bidean-nam-Bian from ridge over Glencoe

51 Aonach Eagach from ridge over Glencoe

52 Glencoe from ridge

53 Snow cornice—Bidean-nam-Bian

54 Loch Etive from Bidean-nam-Bian

55 View towards Buachaille Etives from Bidean-nam-Bian

56 Loch Linnhe from above Banavie

57 Glen Nevis

58 Glen Nevis and Sgùrr a'Mhaim

60 Ben Nevis—Snow Cornice

62 Ben Nevis

63 Glen Nevis

glen like this without damage to the scenery. No doubt it is a convenience to tourists, and the road round Loch Leven makes accessible some splendid country, while one concession has been made, that bridges and culverts are of stone instead of concrete, and so will tone down more quickly to their surroundings. Perhaps in the lower part of the valley, when trees and vegetation have grown up alongside, no irreparable harm has been done, but at the head of the pass, where a way has had to be blasted through the rocks of the gorge, very serious damage has been wrought just at the finest part. In any case, there can have been no financial justification for the extravagance of building a road like this. There is very little traffic: there is the railway to the quarries, and the aluminium works at Kinlochleven are served by boat. The distances from any centre of population are too great to make charabanc tours profitable, and a twentieth part of the money spent on resurfacing the old road would have sufficed for the ordinary tourist motor traffic, especially as visitors ought to wish to drive slowly through the grandest parts of the country they have come so far to see. We ought to take warning from what has so often happened, in the Alps and elsewhere, where mountain railways and other facilities for visiting beauty-spots have resulted in destroying the very beauties they were designed to make accessible. The Mentenvers railway, for instance, at Chamonix was made to enable people to visit one of the grandest spots in the Alps, and if it had stopped discreetly in a hollow just below the summit it would have been entirely justified, but instead it is carried right over the edge of the cliff overlooking the glacier on a great viaduct, and the station with its sordid adjuncts defiles the chief point of vantage, forcing lovers of nature undefiled to clamber some distance to a less perfect viewpoint in order to obtain a true impression of the grandeur of the mountain architecture. On Snowdon the railway wisely stopped a little short of the summit, but we have allowed the finest spot in Wales to be so defiled by squalid drinking-sheds[1] that any true mountain lover is forced to give the summit a wide berth and hurry on to one of the lesser peaks.

In these degenerate days of spoon-fed democracy it is useless to protest against extravagance if it involves spending money on local labour, but when it is too late we shall wake up to the fact that we have got our sense of values all wrong, and that we have sacrificed our priceless heritage of beauty for a mess of pottage.

Returning to Glencoe, about a mile above Clachaig there is the wild little Loch Achtriochtan, beneath the beetling crags of the rock-ridges of Aonach Eagach (47), while on the other side one of the fine peaks of Bidean-nam-Bian stands up grandly between its rocky buttresses.

About three miles farther on the old road climbs up to a rocky barrier called the Study, above the new road gash, which is the finest place from which to see the great buttresses of Bidean-nam-Bian, sometimes called the Three Sisters, whose vast rock precipices give so much character to this part of the glen.

[1] These have now mostly been cleared away to the great benefit of the scene.

The summit ridge of Bidean is better seen by climbing a few hundred feet up the opposite side of the glen (48), where the slope, though steep, is more practicable than lower down, where it is broken by crags and precipices. My most successful expedition in these parts was made by following up this slope to the top of the ridge shutting in Glencoe from the north. It was one of those unsettled days when some of the most glorious effects may be encountered. The sun was shining brightly out of a blue sky flecked with white clouds when we started our climb, but gradually a dark cloud formed above us, and as we reached the top of the ridge we were met with a furious snow-squall, through which, as the snowflakes thinned, the mountains of the Mamore Forest loomed mysteriously. The shower passed quickly, and it was not long before the sun came out again and enabled us to push on along the ridge, enjoying superb views all the way as little snow-showers and brilliant sunshine swiftly followed one another in quick succession, and we were treated to a series of glorious cloud effects as the storm rolled over the snowy mountain-tops, which were alternately glittering in the sunshine and frowning in the majesty of the storm. Beyond the Mamore heights rose the great white mass of Ben Nevis, with the cloud just resting on its topmost snows: to the right came the sharp rocky arête leading up to Carn-Mòr-Dearg, and then the snowy dome of the Aonachs, with the white tent-like peak of Binnein-Mòr, shown on the extreme right of our picture (49). Looking back across the deep trench of Glencoe, the crags and precipices of Bidean-nam-Bian rose majestically, backed by brilliant sunlit clouds (50), while right ahead the curving ridges led on to the crowning heights of Aonach Eagach (3,188 feet), whose rocky bulk stood up finely against the light and dark of the snow-clouds, with the more distant peaks of Ben Vair (3,362 feet) looking over its shoulder (51). At our feet little Loch Achtriochtan was gleaming like a polished mirror in the depths of Glencoe, so brightly that we could hardly look at it, while the sun illuminating the edges of the heavy cloud over Ben Vair added a sparkle and brilliance to the landscape which was enhanced by the cornices and patches of snow of the foreground (52).

We might have continued our walk over Aonach Eagach and come down near the entrance to Glencoe, but the time was getting late, weather was doubtful if beautiful, and we were not sure that there might not be some obstacles on the route if there were much snow in some of the narrow places. We decided therefore to take our time and enjoy the splendid weather effects, which could hardly have been better wherever we could have gone, and to return by the way we had come. We had not reached any famous summit, the highest point being merely marked 2,938 feet on the map, but we had enjoyed views which will mark this as a red-letter day in our holiday annals. It was a good example of the way in which mere aimless rambling may be rewarded. We had started off with the idea of exploring the upper part of the glen, and were then tempted by what looked like a less formidable slope up to the ridge, which formed no part of our original plan, but we hoped to get a better view of the peaks of Bidean-nan-Bian by climbing a little above the road, and as this improved the higher we went we were led on to the ridge, where the swift weather contrasts produced the pageant described in the preceding paragraphs. In future, visitors who are shocked by the gashes made for the new road will be well advised to follow in our footsteps—at any rate sufficiently far to get away from the mess and to see Glencoe in its proper proportions.

The chief ascent from Clachaig is, of course, that of Bidean-nam-Bian (3,766 feet), the crowning height of Argyll, and the highest peak south of the Ben Nevis range, with the exception of Ben Lawers, Ben More, and Stobinian. There is no gentle route to the top, as the mountain, where not precipitous, is excessively steep on all sides. The simplest way is to cross the stream behind the inn and climb straight up the steep buttress labelled An-t-Sron on the one-inch map. It is a tedious pull, but once the ridge overlooking the corrie between this and Stob-Coire-nan-Lochan, the second peak of the mountain, is reached, the hard work has been done and the rest of the walk is full of interest. In one or two places the ridge leading to the summit looked formidable with its snowy covering, but proved quite simple when we reached the spot, though here and there it seemed wise to keep away from the edge of such a snow-cornice as is shown in (53). In this picture the black rocky ridge in the middle distance is that of Aonach Eagach, on the north side of Glencoe; beyond this are the heights of the Mamore Forest, with Ben Nevis and the other big mountains of the range fading into the clouds.

Unfortunately we were not favoured with such brilliant weather as we had encountered on the heights on the opposite side of the glen. It was bright enough when we started, but gradually clouded over, and as it proved beyond us to hurry up the steep part of the ascent the sunshine had gone out of the sky by the time we reached the summit. However, things might have been much worse: even a clouded sky is better for photographic purposes than a perfectly clear one, and too fine a day, especially if there is a tendency to haze, is the next worst condition from this point of view to a definitely bad day of rain and drizzle. The rain held off and the snow on the foreground and on the distant peaks helped to supply some of the contrasts which were otherwise lacking, and if the pictures did not come up to those of the other expedition they did at any rate give some indication of the view. Perhaps the most striking view was that to the south, where Loch Etive divides the hill ranges and adds that contrast to the scene which only a large expense of water can give (54). The fine snowy mountain seen over the loch is Cruachan (3,689 feet), the monarch of all the country round Oban and Loch Awe, while the nearer and more massive hill in the middle distance is Ben Starav (3,541 feet). To the west, variety is given by Loch Leven and Loch Linnhe, and to the east, beyond the snowy ridges and secondary peaks of Bidean itself, are a series of crumpled hills, which are the Buachaille Etives, or Etive Shepherds, whose final crags tower over the upper reach of the glen where it opens out towards Rannoch Moor, and which afford such splendid opportunities to the climbing fraternity of killing themselves or getting into difficulties in these formidable cracks and buttresses. Beyond the broad expanse of the moor the distant Grampians lead the eye into the far distance (55). We made our descent by the back of the mountain, which we found fully as steep as the way by which we had come. It was a relief to be going downhill instead of up, but even so a long slope at such an angle can be very trying to the knees and ankles, and we were not sorry to reach the gentler slopes at the bottom of the glen, even though we had to cover two or three miles of stony or boggy ground.

The Glencoe mountains can be explored also from Kingshouse Inn, situated at the extreme east end of the glen, where the country opens out, but this is really best for the Buachaille Etives, and is therefore perhaps more attractive to active climbers than to the mountain rambler. Kinlochleven might also be a good centre if one could reconcile oneself to making an industrial township into a holiday headquarters. There is fine country all round, and this would probably be the best point from which to explore the fine peaks of the Mamore Forest if the stalking season could be avoided. An Gruagaichean (3,442 feet) is perhaps the most accessible. It commands fine views of the Ben Nevis range to the north, of the Glencoe mountains to the south, and a vista along Loch Leven to the west.

Glencoe and many of the surrounding heights, including Bidean-nam-Bian itself, now belong to the National Trust for Scotland. Walkers and climbers therefore now have free access to this noble stretch of country, which forms a pioneer national park. Perhaps some day we may see the Mamore Forest and Ben Nevis added to it on the north.

A visit to Ben Nevis is the indispensable climax for anyone interested in this part of the country. Not only is it the highest point in Britain, but, in spite of a certain humpiness of shape at the back, it has a range of crags which have few rivals in the country. Fort William, the starting-point, is a town of little interest in itself, situated at the head of Loch Linnhe, where it bends round to form Loch Eil, at the entrance to the Great Glen, through which runs the Caledonian Canal.

The position is well shown in our photograph (56), taken from a hill above Banavie. The town occupies the rising ground on the left of the picture above the flats where the River Lochy discharges its waters into the sea. A portion of the canal is seen in the middle, half-hidden by the heather in the foreground, and Loch Eil comes in on the right. The snow mountains rising over the hills behind the town are the peaks of Ben Vair (Beinn a' Bheithir, 3,362 feet), which guard the entrance to Loch Leven opposite Ballachulish.

Fort William is not an ideal centre for a long stay as it is rather deficient in short walks suitable for doubtful weather, but the longer expeditions rank among the finest in the kingdom.

Glen Nevis is certainly one of the most beautiful valleys in Scotland. It consists of three sections, all of which are first-class examples of their own particular type of scenery. The lower valley is broad, contains some farms and cultivated land, and the river, for the most part, flows gently between wooded banks fringed with trees.[1] Ben Nevis presents its dull side to the valley, but the heights of the Mamore Forest on the other side have a broken and varied outline, and look very impressive when there is plenty of snow about (57, 58). Sgùrr a'Mhaim (3,601 feet) has a cap of white quartzite, giving it almost the look of a snow mountain even in the summer, when the real snows have all melted.

About five miles from Fort William the valley bends round, and the second section of the glen is entered. This is entirely wild and filled with rocks, whilst trees crown every crag and eminence. Fine and rugged specimens of the beautiful Scots pine, with red bark and blue-green foliage, can be found here in abundance (59), and the river tumbles in a series of cataracts through a rocky gorge.

Two or three miles farther on the valley bends again and ascends by a wild rocky gorge (63) to the desolate upland country beyond, hemmed in by lofty peaks. Just beyond the gorge a fine waterfall descends from the mountain, closing the view at the end.

The ordinary ascent of Ben Nevis (4,406 feet) is by a pony track which avoids all difficulties, and conducts the climber by easy gradients to the top.

In the snowy spring of 1922, however, conditions were very different, and we found it quite an arduous enterprise. Deep snow began at the half-way hut and the path was entirely obliterated, while the obvious route across certain hollows was blocked by heavy cornices of snow, forcing us to make a more or less direct ascent of the steep snow slopes instead of following the gentler summer route. Stumbling over half-buried rocks and plunging through deep snow is a particularly tiring sort of exercise, and we were very glad to reach the ridge, from a projecting spur of which we had a fine view of the tremendous precipices of the northern face (62).

All along the top the edge was heavily corniced (60), making great care necessary when approaching anywhere near the edge. The last part of the walk was less steep but was quite hard enough work in the deep loose snow, especially as the weather was looking doubtful, with occasional clouds and snow flurries which made it necessary to hurry for fear of losing our way back. If a thick mist had settled down it might have been easy to go astray, for the wind was blowing little drifts of snow from the cliffs across the mountain, quickly obliterating the tracks we had made on the way up.

The snow on the top must have been exceedingly deep, as we suddenly found ourselves walking over the roof of the little inn which serves summer visitors with refreshments, the only sign of the building being a chimney-pot pushing up through the snow.

The view from the top is very extensive, but I sometimes think that the view from the highest summit loses something by the mere fact that one is looking down on everything. Mountains are apt to fall short of their full dignity when looked down upon, and an uninterrupted series of lesser heights stretching away as far as the eye can reach may become monotonous in the absence of any striking or pre-eminent object. A stretch of water sometimes

[1] There has recently been some encroachment here by the Forestry Commission.

gives the necessary contrast, as in the view from Cruachan shown in (31), and Loch Eil serves something of the same purpose in the panorama from Ben Nevis, though the surrounding hills are less striking.

The most effective thing, however, on this occasion was the view of the snow-covered heights of the Mamore Forest (61), the highest peak of which is Binnein Mor (3,700 feet). Bidean-nam-Bian (3,766 feet) and the other Glencoe mountains were also fine objects rising over the intervening ridges. In the deep snow, with all Scotland lying at our feet and soft mists drifting over the landscape and occasionally enveloping us in their folds, we felt wonderfully remote from the busy world in which we spend most of our lives. It is good at times to go up into the hills, like the prophets of old, and there, alone with the clouds of heaven above us and the noblest of terrestrial forms at our feet, to imbibe something of the spirit of infinity and worship before the throne of the Creator of them in humility and awe!

The best and most comprehensive view of the precipices of Ben Nevis is obtained from Carn Mor Dearg (4,012 feet), the mountain immediately opposite to the crags on the north-east. Extensive bogs have first to be crossed till a fine glimpse of the great rock wall is obtained from the mouth of the corrie beneath it, and then the opposite ridge has to be attacked. This is not particularly steep, and leads straight up to the top of the mountain.

The sharp summit (64) is an impressive object when covered deeply with snow, but is far less formidable than it looks. The top of Ben Nevis towers up grandly directly opposite (65), looking very different from the rounded hump it appears to be on the other side.

Under the wintry conditions prevailing when these photographs were taken, the cliffs rose up magnificently from the snow-filled corrie, their edges picked out by a long, sharply cut cornice of deep snow. The distant view across the Mamore Forest mountains was also most impressive, the sharp snow-covered ridges in the foreground giving a very Alpine appearance (66).

Another most excellent walk from Fort William is to follow the road up the glen a little more than half-way along the first section, and then to turn to the right and climb the hills on the south side. Antiquaries may find an interesting vitrified fort on an eminence commanding a pass over into the next valley, and, just beyond this, a ridge begins leading up to Mullach-nan-Coirean (3,077 feet), the first of the bigger mountains shutting in the head of the glen.

We chose a day of uncertain weather for this expedition, as we were waiting for a more settled day for Ben Nevis itself, and had to spend a good deal of time crouching under rocks to get out of the icy blasts of wind that dashed hailstones and snow flurries into our faces. But the sun came out brilliantly between the showers, and the contrast between the blue sky and furious stormclouds produced many beautiful and striking effects.

Plate 67 shows a particularly angry-looking snowstorm advancing upon us from the hills beyond Loch Linnhe. We felt a little nervous in our exposed position at the sight of this black column of cloud coming straight at us, and hastily sought out holes in the rocks in which to take cover, but it passed over in time like the others, the hail mostly bouncing off us without wetting our clothes, and the sun came out again more brilliantly than before. As the storm approached the clouds formed a complete arch across the sky of inky black vapour, under which the sun could be seen shining quietly in the fine interval beyond.

These conditions may mean a little discomfort while one is waiting for the hail to pass over, but they are extraordinarily beautiful, and give the photographer chances which seldom come to him in finer and more settled weather.

After the storm had passed we were able to proceed to the top of our mountain, obtaining several very beautiful views of snow ridges and gleaming waters, backed by glorious clouds sailing across the blue. They were especially fine when looking down the long stretch of Loch Linnhe (68) and, farther south, towards the grand peaks of Ben Vair over Ballachulish (69).

ABOUT FOUR MILES ALONG THE road to Fort William, from Ballachulish Ferry, Loch Linnhe narrows down to a channel little more than a quarter of a mile wide, through which the tide swirls at a considerable pace. At Corran Narrows, as the place is called, there is a ferry, with a comfortable little hotel on the opposite side. The ferry-boat is not large enough for motor-cars, and they have to go round by Fort William and both sides of Loch Eil, a distance of some forty miles, half of it by a road on which motorists are warned to use special care owing to the narrowness, sharp corners, and poor surface of the way. Ardgour is therefore a fairly peaceful resort, and is less generally known than it deserves to be.

A curious low-lying flat, about two and a half miles long by one deep, is stretched out between the Narrows and the steep hills. It is well wooded, with one or two good houses, and a little village straggling along a beech avenue, while the views across the water are naturally very fine. But the best views are obtained about three miles along the road on each side of the hotel, where it passes beyond the flats and runs round the base of the mountain barriers shutting in the deep depression of Glen Gour. Here the slopes are well wooded, mostly with native birch, and the shores are rocky, with romantic little bays and coves. Going in the northerly direction the peaks of Beinn a'Bheithir (Ben Vair, 3,367 feet) stand up splendidly across the water (70).

About two miles from Corran Ben Nevis itself becomes the chief feature, and is best seen just before the road turns inland in order to pass round Inverscaddle Bay (71). The monarch of Scottish hills (4,406 feet) has the reputation of being rather a shapeless hump when seen from anywhere except opposite the great northern precipices, but from here it stands up magnificently above all the surrounding hills, supported by two broad shoulders, and if its stature is emphasized, as in our picture, by a mantle of snow gleaming in the sunshine, it fully deserves its title. On a bright spring day, with white clouds in a blue sky, whose shadows are chasing one another across the landscape, the blue waters of the loch, and the fresh green of the early foliage just beginning to show and sparkle in the sunshine, the distant snows complete the picture in a very perfect manner, and add a touch of almost indescribable beauty. In fact one member of our party actually complained that the scene was too ideally perfect, too much what Scottish

64 Carn Mor Dearg

65 Ben Nevis from Carn-Mòr-Dearg

66 View from Carn-Mòr-Dearg

67 Hailstorm from Mullach-nan-Coirean

68 Loch Linnhe from Mullach-nan-Coirean

Ben Weir from Mullach nan Coirean

70 Beinn a'Bheithir (Ben Vair) from Ardgour

71 Ben Nevis from near Inverscaddle

72 Ben Nevis from near Inverscaddle

73 Sgùrr Dhomhnuill from Glen Scaddle

74 Ben Nevis from Glen Scaddle

75 Ben Nevis from Ben Keil

76 Loch Leven from Ben Keil

77 Glen Gour

78 View across Loch Linnhe

79 Ben Nevis from Sgùrr Dhomhnuill

80 Loch Sunart and Garbh-bheinn

I

81 Loch Sunart from South Shore

82 Coire-an-Iubhair

83 Garbh-bheinn—Summit

84 View from Garbh-bheinn

85 Ben Resipol from Garbh-bheinn

86 Glen Strontian

87 Loch Sunart—a Stormy Evening

scenery ought to be for it to be real! It was the same feeling which has caused people I have known to stand and laugh at the Matterhorn for being so ridiculously like the beau-ideal of a Swiss Alpine peak, or which sometimes causes the visitor to weary of contemplating the perfection of a picture by Raphael because there is nothing he can criticize.

Another photograph of Ben Nevis, taken from a little nearer Corran with a long-focus lens, brings out its stature more fully (72), though the absence of the shoulder on the right, hidden behind the nearer hill, rather spoils the grace of its outline.

It is well worth while to follow the foot-track up Glen Scaddle for two or three miles. It runs beside a delightful little river, which here and there has to cut its way through rocky dykes which form rapids and little waterfalls and enchanting pools. At the head of the glen the graceful peak of Sgùrr Dhomhnuill (2,915 feet), the crowning summit of Ardgour, closes the vista most satisfactorily (73), while in the other direction the snowy dome of Ben Nevis towers over the tree-tops about twelve miles away (74). Those who wish to appreciate the great mountain should not content themselves with looking up at the foreshortened views from the neighbourhood of Fort William, but should either go to the hollow below the great northern crags or, still better, climb to the top of Carn-Mòr-Dearg opposite, or else ferry over to the west side of Loch Linnhe and get far enough away to enable them to take in its proper proportions.

A bird's-eye view of exceptional beauty may be obtained from the hill above this bit of road. I believe it is called Ben Keil locally, from the farmhouse at its foot, but the Ordnance Map gives it the unpronounceable name of Sgùrr-na-h'Eanchainne, and dubs the next one to it Beinn-na-Cille, suggesting that Keil is a corruption of Cille, 'church', from the little graveyard at its foot. This is the best point from which to start the ascent, as it is not quite so steep as the slope facing Corran, and we found it fairly dry and good going, so that the climb was not too toilsome if not too hurried. Hence Ben Nevis stands up grandly, with the snow reflected in the loch below (75).

But the view across the entrance to Loch Leven to the mountains above Glencoe was even more beautiful, with the snow picking out the higher peaks and the blue water winding away far into their recesses (76). The junction of Loch Leven with Loch Linnhe lay at our feet, with the Ballachulish straits slightly to the left, and the shapely peaks of Ben Vair towering above. Farther away, to the left, was the great bulk of Bidean-nam-Bian (3,766 feet), with its black precipices dropping away into a corrie, beyond which the second peak, Stob-Coire-nan-Lochan (3,657 feet) raised its white pyramid into the sunshine. Our hill reached the height of 2,397 feet, which is sufficient to command a very wide prospect, especially across so great an expanse of water, and it is a fact that the best views are not always from the highest peaks, as a mountain looked up at is more imposing than one looked down upon. Ben Keil is connected at the back with a massive hill, which curves round to a lower ridge and provides an alternative descent, though

1*

this proved so steep in places that we were glad that we had not reversed our route. We had arrived at the top in brilliant weather, and congratulated ourselves on reaching so fine a viewpoint under perfect conditions, but after spending some time on the summit a curious gloom began to work up from the south, into which the mountains gradually faded until their snowy tops alone loomed like ghosts through the haze. This meant no more photographs, and portended a change of weather, though this came so slowly that we did not have to use undue haste on our return journey.

Three miles to the south-west of the Corran Narrows the road skirts the base of steep hills, and after crossing the river by a bridge, from which there is an excellent view up Glen Gour (77), for some three miles until it turns into Glen Tarbert the way is one of the prettiest drives in Britain. The shores are rocky, with little inlets and islands, and are clothed in native wood sufficiently open to give a series of delightful glimpses of the mountains on the opposite shore. These are broken up by the deep recesses of Loch Leven and Glencoe, while farther off the gleam of the distant snows of the Mamore Forest and of Ben Nevis add a touch of brillaince to the fairyland of birch, bracken, and water of the foreground (78). This was indeed a place in which to dally and enjoy the changing lights thrown over the landscape by an April sky.

The hill above is worth climbing for the sake of the view across the loch, and if the walk is prolonged across a bumpy waste as far as the edge overlooking Coire-an-Iubhair there is a very fine view of the grim crags of Garbh-bheinn on the other side. On the occasion of our visit we had spent so long enjoying the exquisite beauty of the woods by the shore of the loch that we had to content ourselves with a rather distant view of Garbh-bheinn, especially as the weather was beginning to show signs of breaking up. But a further exploration of this ridge and a nearer approach to the precipices would obviously reward the rambler with a little more time on his hands.

Glen Tarbert is a deep V-shaped depression cut right through the hills, affording passage-way for the road to Loch Sunart, which nowhere has to climb above 450 feet over sea-level. It is a gloomy and forbidding pass, hemmed in by great walls of naked rock, mostly too steep to offer a practicable ascent but not precipitous enough to strike the imagination, while the summit crags are hidden by their massive supports. The first time we drove through we were greeted by a furious snowstorm, which decidedly increased the wild desolation of the scene. It came down so hard that we had to stop and clear the windscreen every minute or two, and progress was so slow that we began to wonder whether we should ever get through; but it stopped at last, and it was a pleasant relief to see the bright waters of Loch Sunart ahead and less furious weather prevailing over the lower seaward ranges.

There is an excellent little inn at Strontian, situated in a wooded bay about a mile and a half from the head of the loch. We found it unpretentious but very efficiently managed, and it is the best headquarters from which to explore this fine district, as the four chief mountains are all most conveniently reached from it. There are also pleasant drives or walks along both sides of the loch and for some distance up the broad Strontian valley. At the head of this there were some ancient deserted mines, and the rough roads leading up to these provide an easy route through what might have been a trackless and swampy country. One of these goes over a pass 1,100 or 1,200 feet high to Loch Doilet, said to be a famous fishing loch, whose shores are being thickly planted by the Forestry Commission, and thence there is a pleasant walk through Polloch to the birch-clad shores of Loch Shiel, which forms the north-western boundary of our district. Hence there is a delightful glimpse of some of the fine mountains about Glenfinnan at the head of this long and narrow loch (99).

If I contemplate a visit of some days' duration I like to select a place with a broad outlook across the water, because in unsettled or stormy weather, when it is too bad for excursions into the higher hills, there is usually something to watch—a temporary break in the storm-clouds with the light piercing the gloom and reflected in the water, or some of those fascinating clearing-up effects after heavy rain. Strontian cannot compete with Ballachulish as such a weather observatory, for the mountains beyond the loch lack both height and outline as compared with those across Loch Linnhe, but it is not a bad spot for the purpose, as the aspect of the bay changes quickly as the tide rises and falls, and there are good short walks along the shores for the finer intervals. During our stay we met with all kinds of weather, with no two days alike, and there were plenty of opportunities for lying in wait with a camera to catch the varied effects of sunshine and shower. On one day especially the clouds were most magnificent, when their shining masses were swept aside by a strong breeze and their sharp edges stood out clear-cut against the pure blue of the rain-washed sky, except where a shower cast a grey shadow across the distance. That same evening there were some grand effects as the sun sank into heavy banks of cloud whose dark forms, sharply defined in the brilliantly clear atmosphere, were reflected in the smooth water of the bay (2). Another evening a great black storm-cloud swept up across the mountains and quickly obscured the last golden light of the setting sun with its threatening pall of vapour, presage of a wild night on the hills (87).

The best views of Loch Sunart are obtained from the road along the opposite side of the water which eventually makes its way over the hills to join the highway to Loch Aline on the Sound of Mull. For the first part of the walk the chief feature is Garbh-bheinn, less impressive from this side as the famous crags turn their back on us, but quite imposing after a fresh sprinkle of snow with the dark snowcloud passing away over Glen Tarbert (80). The shores are rocky, and at low tide especially the rocks and seaweed provide a good foreground, while farther on the road climbs through birch-woods, with delightful glimpses of the hills across the water seen framed in their feathery branches. After three or four miles from the head of the loch the road turns inland, but a branch continues for a mile or two more to a large private house. It is worth while to follow this for some way for the sake of the fine view of the range of hills forming the backbone of Ardgour, which raises a broken outline beyond and above the lower hills over Strontian on the opposite side of the loch (81). Seen as we saw them on a bright unsettled day, with the loftier peaks and ridges picked out by fresh-fallen snow, the long white range from the bulky Garbh-bheinn on the right to the shapely pyramid of Sgùrr Dhomhnuill on the left, they had a suggestion of the Alps as viewed from the northern shores of the Lake of Lucerne, though in Scotland the foreground is wilder and evidences of man's handiwork less obtrusive.

Though on a comparatively small scale, the four chief mountains of this district are peculiarly attractive to the mountaineer. Although none of them quite attain the dignity of 3,000 feet in height, which the Scottish Mountaineering Club seems to regard as a qualification for the very name of 'mountain', even their guide-book is constrained to describe Garbh-bheinn as one of the finest hills in Scotland. Its great eastern precipices abound in chimneys and buttresses, which provide numerous sensational climbs for the rock enthusiast, and fill up several pages in the *Mountaineering Club Guide*. In addition to the interest of the mountains themselves, they are so situated as to command some of the finest views in the Highlands. Nothing sets off or gives such a variety to a mountain landscape as the presence of large sheets of water, and from all these hills we seem almost surrounded by great lochs winding away from beneath our feet into the dim distance. The sea-lochs of Linnhe, Sunart, and Moidart, and the long narrow freshwater Loch Shiel, shut them in on all sides, and beyond these on a clear day is the distant gleam of the open sea, dotted with islands like Rum and Eigg, whose distinctive outlines attract attention even at their extreme distance. Added to this the mountains of Sunart are situated right opposite to some of the grandest peaks of the Highlands, which form a splendid background in the east.

Our first attempt on Garbh-bheinn (2,903 feet) was a failure. The best route is to drive, or take the morning mail-car, almost to the bridge over the stream coming down from the wild Coire-an-Iubhair into Glen Tarbert, and then to climb up the rocky ridge on the west side of the corrie. On this occasion we got up to about 1,000 feet, but were met by such a violent and cold gale, and such threatening clouds gathering to windward, that we decided it was a day for valleys rather than hills, and came down and explored the wild Coire-an-Iubhair, which curls round under the crags of Garbh-bheinn. This is one of the wildest and most desolate corries to be found outside Skye, and if more accessible would have a bigger reputation. The walk along the bottom is boggy and tiresome, but we had to push on far enough to get round the corner which hid the big precipices from the mouth of the corrie. The upper part is almost all bare rock, and the vast crags towering up above us, with the cloud-wrack playing about their jagged summits, were most impressive in the dull conditions prevailing (82). Remembering the bogs we had come through we were not anxious to retrace our steps, and therefore decided to brave the weather and cross the pass at the head of the corrie, returning by the Gleann Feith-n'Amean on the north side of the mountain to Loch Sunart. From the head of the pass we looked down on what appeared to be a dreary stretch of bog reaching all down the valley, and as sleet had begun to fall the prospects for the rest of the walk did not look very inviting. However, the showers seemed to hesitate about descending from the hills, and we found that if we followed closely the bank of the stream there was usually a narrow strip drained by it, by which we made better progress than we had expected. To follow the windings of the river made a very considerable increase in the distance to be covered, but the drier track made our progress much more rapid.

Our second attack on Garbh-bheinn was much more successful. As before, we took the mail-car to the bridge and climbed up by the same ridge. It proved fairly free from bog, while the rocky outcrops made it an interesting scramble, and the views improved at every step. About two-thirds of the way up there is a fairly level kind of platform, where the bare rocks serve as an admirable set-off to the splendid view across Loch Linnhe. Garbh-bheinn is the finest belvedere of the district, as it commands a nearer view of Loch Linnhe than most of its rivals, and there are fewer intervening ridges between it and the water. Loch Leven comes into Loch Linnhe just opposite, enclosed by the heights over Glencoe, and the white line of the Mamore Forest peaks peers over the ridges on the left in a most attractive way. From the top of the ridge just before it turns to join the great ridge there is a very good view of the summit and of the precipices of the eastern face, besides a more distant glimpse of the ranges beyond, among which the shapely peak of Sgùrr Dhomhnuill stands up finely (83). The final ascent to the top from this point does not take long, and the view looking down over the crags to Loch Linnhe, Loch Leven, Ben Vair, and Glencoe must be one of the finest in all Scotland (84). We had arrived in unsettled weather, with fine clouds and considerable periods of sunshine—conditions most favourable for a Highland landscape—but after we had watched it with great pleasure for some time a series of little snow-showers began to beat up from the distance. One of these enveloped us on our mountain-top, but as there was not much wind with it we were able to wrap ourselves in our mackintoshes and sit through it without great discomfort, and when it passed it was very interesting to watch the grand effects as it cleared and other little showers drifted across the hills. They rather interrupted the view of Ben Nevis, but that to the north and west comprised an enormous number of hills: most striking of all was Ben Resipol (2,774 feet), whose isolated position makes it a conspicuous landmark from all the country round. Its rocky ridge seen from either end forms a sharp pyramid, and it looked very fine when it emerged from a fierce snow-shower with the sun shining on the sea beyond and a towering mass of cloud cumulus above its peak (85). A return to Strontian may be made by the long ridge which bounds Glen Tarbert and descends over a number of minor peaks and swellings to the head of Loch Sunart. Few hills in Scotland have more to offer to the rambler and lover of mountain scenery, as well as to the rock-climber.

Sgùrr Dhomhnuill (2,915 feet) is the highest mountain of the Ardgour group, overtopping Garbh-bheinn, according to the Ordnance Survey, by 12 feet. Its graceful peak, flanked by a lower but also pointed spur on the south side, gives it a characteristic outline whether seen from the Strontian Glen and Loch Sunart (86) or from Glen Scaddle (73). Though it lacks the magnificent crags and precipices which make Garbh-bheinn one of the grandest of the lesser mountains of Scotland, it is a very interesting ascent and a particularly fine viewpoint. On the map the walk from Strontian looks rather a long one, as it is five or six miles to the beginning of the climb, but the walk up the valley is a very pleasant one, at first through a wide fertile strath watered by a fair-sized river, backed by the fine outline of our mountain (86), then through open woods by an old miners' road, which neglect has rendered hardly suitable for wheeled traffic, but which provides an almost ideal path for the pedestrian and enables him to cover the distance with ease and comfort in much less time than would be required for the usual rough cross-country track. As will be gathered from our illustration, Sgùrr Dhomhnuill is in the shape of a great horseshoe, with the peak in the middle and long ridges stretching out on each side. At the foot of the nearer black ridge the track stops at some deserted mine-workings, and here, instead of following the *Mountaineering Club Guide's* instructions to proceed up the corrie between the two ridges, it is better to cross the stream and mount the nearer ridge, in order to avoid bogs. A ridge walk is always more interesting and therefore less tiring than one along the bottom, and when the base of the little peak in which the ridge culminates is reached, a kind of nick or corridor will be found leading directly and easily to the bealach, or col, between the lesser peak and the main summit. Here there are springs of clear water and an excellent place to stop for lunch before making the final ascent. The latter from this point is not long, and consists of a couple of steep pitches with a kind of platform between the two, which, as is often the case, may provide better foregrounds for the photographer than the narrower summit. We were favoured with brilliantly clear weather, and the views in all directions were superb. We even claimed to make out the white line of the Cairngorms, seventy miles away. The view of the Glencoe hills is not so fine as that from Garbh-bheinn, for Loch Linnhe is farther away and only little peeps of it can be obtained, as it is mostly cut off by the intervening ranges, but Ben Nevis towers up splendidly some seventeen or eighteen miles away, at the end of the long vista of Glen Scaddle (79). The white tops of the Mamore Forest heights on the right also look very attractive. Nearer, the dark crags of Garbh-bheinn are rather forbidding, although from this point we look at the back of the precipices, while behind them in the distance the faint glimmer of the snows of Cruachan can usually be clearly made out. To the west the view is better than from Garbh-bheinn, as we are nearer the sea. Ben Resipol stands up well in its isolation, with the lower reaches of Loch Shiel and Loch Moidart at its foot, while beyond is the distant gleam of the sea, with Rum, Eigg, and the other islands. To the north, range beyond range of mountains lead the eye away to Scour Ouran and Carn Eige for forty or fifty miles of confused ridges and peaks, whose identification is a fascinating game to the possessor of a field-glass, but which would hardly be effective in a photograph.

The mountain bounding Glen Tarbert on the south side is Creach-bheinn (2,800 feet). It is not so imposing as the last two described above, but possesses some quite good rocks and corries, and is well worth climbing for the sake of the view. It was selected as a station for the trigonometrical survey by the Ordnance Map authorities, and traces of the wall built to protect their encampment are still to be seen in a hollow just below the summit. From Strontian the route is fairly obvious: a cart road, leading to a farm, strikes off just beyond the bridge, saving the first half-mile of bog, and another two-thirds of a mile of sloppy walking, part of which may be dodged by keeping to the river bank, brings one to a stream which comes tumbling down the hillside from the moorland to the west of Creach-bheinn. If this is crossed the ascent can be made through the birch-wood on the farther bank, on reaching the top of which the way follows the ridge until it turns right to the main ridge leading up to the summit. For a large part of the way a kind of natural corridor drained by a small stream provides an excellent route, with an intermittent path, and there is water to drink all the way up to the final ridge. This is useful as providing numerous sites for an early lunch, but experienced mountaineers will refrain from drinking too frequently while going uphill, as it only increases thirst.

We started for Creach-bheinn on a warm morning, and for the first part of the climb, with the sun beating down on us, it seemed the hottest day of the holiday, but when we were on the top it turned to the coldest, as we met a piercing wind driving snow-showers before it. It is well, therefore, especially early in the year, to retain fairly warm clothing, or at any rate to carry a light wrap. We needed our mackintoshes that day for the sake of their warmth as well as a protection against the snow. I hope my readers are not bored by these personal experiences in a commonplace walk, where there is no adventure or difficulty to give interest to the story, but I give them in the hope that these individual recollections may give a somewhat more vivid touch to my descriptions, and make it easier to realize the conditions under which the accompanying illustrations were obtained.

From the corner where the ridge turns in the view begins to open up, and the bare rocks of Garbh-bheinn stand up boldly over the desolate hollow at our feet (88), though we are looking only at the back of the mountain, whose grand crags are facing the other way. The view from the top is very extensive, though the lower spurs of the mountain cut off some of the water which would have greatly improved the general effect. It was best towards Ben Nevis and the Mamore Forest, and the monarch of Scottish hills, gleaming with snow, asserted its supremacy as usual (89). To the south a greater stretch of water faded away beyond Oban, bounded by the hills of Mull, Jura, and even Arran. It is possible that even finer views might have been obtained from some of the minor peaks or ridges jutting out towards Loch Linnhe, but the weather was showing signs of deterioration, snow-showers were becoming more frequent, we were getting tired of the cold wind, and thought it wiser to make our way down again while there was still a chance of getting back reasonably dry. There were some rather fine effects on the top while we were waiting for the snow-showers to pass over. In the intervals the heavy clouds overhead, with a kind of grey curtain of falling snow drifting across the landscape, leaving glimpses between the veils of distant sea and mountain, formed pictures which we could have stopped to watch indefinitely if it had only been a little warmer (90).

The fourth indispensable ascent from Strontian is that of Ben Resipol (2,774 feet), a particularly attractive little mountain, both from its shape and situation. The walk requires little exertion and is most repaying. The top is a rocky comb, which looks like a sharp peak when seen from either end, and its isolated position makes it a landmark from all the country round. We have seen how it stands up among the lower hills towards the sea from Garbh-bheinn (85). It also commands the middle reaches of Loch Sunart, and is seen at its best from the coast a little to the west of Salen Bay (91).

It is a pleasant walk of ten or eleven miles along the north shore of Loch Sunart to Salen. One doubtful morning we started for this, but when we had gone about half-way the weather looked like improving and we were tempted by an attractive-looking cart-road leading up to a farm called Ardarie, right under Ben Resipol. On reaching the farm we took to the hills, and found a fairly dry route up to a rocky plateau called Beinn-an-Albannaich, which is a very pleasant place to wander about on. It commands fine views, and the rocky outcrops and little tarns—or lochans as I suppose they should be called in Scotland—form an interesting foreground. Skirting one of the largest of these little lakes we found ourselves at the foot of the final cone of Ben Resipol. This is steep, but a way between the rocks can be found almost anywhere, and the rise is not long enough to be exhausting. There is an alternative route from the little inn at Salen, which follows the shore westward for about two and a half miles and then takes a footpath leading on to the hills through the little village of Resipol. A stream is then followed and a plateau is reached on the opposite side of the summit from the last described route. Hence there is a very excellent view over Loch Shiel and of the tangle of hills culminating in the graceful peak of Sgùrr Dhomhnuill. The scramble to the summit rocks is similar to that from the other side. The view is an exceptionally fine one, as there is no rival height in the immediate neighbourhood to interrupt the panorama, and the long winding sea-loch of Sunart on one side and the straight fresh-water Loch Shiel on the other, with Loch Moidart and the sea in the distance, provide the variety which we have again and again pointed out to be one of the chief elements needed for the ideal view, and one very characteristic of the west coast. The view across Sunart is over lower hills, and Mull to the left and Rum to the right are points of interest in the distance. The sea of peaks over and beyond Loch Shiel (92) provide plenty of exercise with map and compass for those geographically minded climbers who like to identify these complicated ranges, while to the east the distant snow of Ben Nevis, looking impossibly high on the day of our visit, towered over Sgùrr Dhomhnuill (93). To the

88 Garbh-bheinn from Creach-bheinn

89　Ben Nevis from Creach-bheinn

90 Snow showers from Creach-bheinn

91　Ben Resipol from Salen

92 Loch Shiel from Ben Resipol

93 View from Ben Resipol

94 Loch Moidart

95 Ben Resipol from Loch Shiel

96 Loch Shiel from Glenfinnan

K

97 Rum from Loch Moidart
98 St. Finnan's Chapel, Loch Shiel

99 Loch Shiel, near Pollock
100 Loch Shiel, from Glenfinnan

101　Ben Hiant from Kilchoan

102 Rum from Beinn-na-Seilg

102 Loch-nan-Uamh, gathering seaweed

104 Morar—Sunset behind Rum

105. Rum from Morar

106 Morar—Sunset behind Showers

107 Morar—Sunset

108 Loch Morar

109 Loch Nevis and Sgùrr na Ciche

110 Loch Nevis—Entrance

111   The Five Sisters from Mam Ratagan

112 Loch Hourn near Arnisdale

113 Loch Hourn—Birch Woods (now destroyed)

114 Loch Hourn and Ben Sgriol

right Garbh-bheinn stood out against a background of threatening cloud, while the jagged rocks and patches of snow made an excellent foil to the prospect. The descent can be made by following the ridge to its eastern extremity, and then dropping steeply down to the path leading from Strontian to Loch Shiel, reaching it almost at the top of the pass. The whole round from Strontian is most enjoyable, and as it is neither too long nor too lofty a climb it is an ideal walk for the middle-aged mountaineer who is no longer anxious to undertake the more strenuous exertions required for higher peaks.

From Salen a road crosses the isthmus between Loch Sunart and Loch Shiel, and in two miles reaches Acharacle, at the foot of the latter, where there is another hotel, which serves as a base for the exploration of this district. It has the disadvantage of a dull flat morass which has to be crossed in order to reach the interesting rocky shores of Loch Moidart, though a road makes this feasible. Once across there are pleasant rambles by the sea, with grand views across to Eigg, with the splendid outlines of the hills of Rum appearing over its lower waist (97). The view landwards past the wooded Shona Islands towards the mountains overlooking Loch Ailort is also very attractive (94). The walk right round the coast from Loch Moidart to Loch Ailort, where the West Highland Railway may be rejoined, is said to be exceptionally beautiful, but as we had fixed our headquarters at Acharacle, and it was much too long to do both ways in a day, I am not able to give first-hand information about it.

The south shore of the lower end of Loch Shiel is also a boggy flat which it would be most wearisome to cross, and this end of the loch can therefore be best explored by boat, landing at the most favourable points, for it is seldom possible to get a satisfactory photograph from a boat, since foregrounds are difficult to arrange and the mountains tend to be dwarfed unless the camera can be brought at any rate a little above the surface of the water. From the pier there is an excellent view of our old friend Resipol, and it was interesting to watch the changing weather effects over his isolated peak. I show a view taken on an uncertain day, with attractive lighting conditions (95).

About five miles up the loch is the sacred isle of St. Finnan, with the ruins of a church said to have been built by the saint himself in the seventh century. The walls are only a few feet high and there are no architectural features to enable one to substantiate the claim to this vast antiquity, especially as the method of building a rough stone wall has hardly changed in this out-of-the-way region in all the twelve hundred years. The island is still used as a burial-ground, and votaries of the rival creeds rest beside one another in this holy ground—Roman Catholics on one side and Presbyterians on the other—both alike claiming the protection of the disciple of Columba (98).

After passing under Ben Resipol there is a fine view up the Polloch Glen, backed by the shapely peaks of Sgùrr Dhomhnuill and its neighbours. After passing this the loch turns in a north-westerly direction, and a long straight reach walled in by steep but rather monotonous mountains proves

L

the least interesting part of the voyage. The finest part is near the head, where deep hollows separate finely peaked mountains. The voyage ends at Glenfinnan, where the memory of the ancient saint has been somewhat effaced by that of a very different person in the shape of Prince Charlie, who gathered the clans together under his standard in this spot in 1745. A rather clumsy pillar commemorates this event. It is difficult to obtain good views in the immediate neighbourhood of Glenfinnan, as private grounds border the road for some distance, but below the church it is possible to get a glimpse of the fine mountains on the east side of the loch (99), and by going a little way along the road towards Loch Eil and climbing a slight eminence there is a good view down the river towards the head of the loch and the fine hills Beinn Odhar Mhòr (2,853 feet) and Beinn Odhar Bheag (2,895 feet), which dominate the west side of the head of Loch Shiel (96). As not unfrequently happens, the 'little ben' turns out to be the higher of the two, but the other is nearer and more bulky. The ascent of these would make a very attractive expedition, but they are outside the limits set down for treatment in this chapter, and it is now time to return to Salen and continue our exploration of the western reaches of Loch Sunart and the less lofty but wild country round Ardnamurchan.

The Loch Shiel steamer is the chief link between Ardnamurchan and the rest of the world, though a steamer plying between Oban and the Outer Hebrides calls at Kilchoan on certain days each week. There is a comfortable little hotel at Kilchoan, which is the best, if not the only, resting-place in the western part of the peninsula. The road from Acharacle through Salen runs for more than half the way along the shores of Loch Sunart before turning inland to avoid Ben Hiant, which blocks the way. The drive is a beautiful one, especially in the neighbourhood of Glenborrodale, where the rather pretentious castle stands in beautiful grounds overlooking a group of hilly islands. For the first part of the way the chief feature is Ben Resipol (91), and about Glenborrodale the coast is broken up into a number of narrow inlets and rocky promontories, covered with rich woods. Where the road turns inland the scenery becomes more severe, though the fine outline of Ben Hiant serves to break the monotony. Trees become scarcer, and one is reminded of some tracts in Ireland. The road is not a modern speed-track, but in spite of narrowness and steep hills and sharp corners is quite safe if the car is driven carefully and at moderate speed, though there are places where if two large cars meet one of them may have to back for some distance before finding a passing-place. The public mail-car, by which we travelled, was an ancient contraption which did the twenty miles or so in under four hours! Each time we came to a hill we thought we should never reach the top, but in spite of its rattles and groans and roars it triumphantly breasted each rise, and brought us to our destination. Coming home it started at about 6 a.m. in order to catch the 10 a.m. boat, and I must confess that we decided to reject the lessons in economy learned from our thrifty Scottish friends and hire a car, which, although none of the most modern, enabled us to breakfast in peace, give the mail two hours' start and arrive at our destination with three-quarters of an hour to spare! Perhaps before these lines are in print the ancient post-office car will be replaced by a more efficient vehicle: it certainly could not be expected to last many more years, but the journey is not one to be hurried over, at any rate in fine weather.

The hotel at Kilchoan is not actually on the sea, but is placed high enough to command a view across the water to the distant hills of Mull. A short road leads down to the coast in ten minutes' walk and ends in a pier, now little used, as the new steamers from Oban cannot come in so close, and land their passengers in the bay by means of rowing-boats. The coast can also be reached half a mile farther on by a branch road leading to the ruined Mingary Castle, which is mentioned in Scott's *Legend of Montrose* as having been seized by the Irish troops under Colkitto in 1645. Loch Sunart has here broadened out to meet the Sound of Mull and we have almost arrived at the open sea. The whole character of the country has changed from the river-like shores of the narrow winding loch to the more open and austere type of the sea-coast. The cliffs for the most part are not very high, but reefs of rock jutting out into the sea add interest, especially at low tide. They are in places divided by long straight bands of hard rock, which appear to be of volcanic origin. Some of these reefs are seen in our photograph looking across the bay towards the entrance to Loch Sunart (101). Ben Hiant presents a fine outline, and makes the most of its moderate height of 1,729 feet, especially when a cloud-wreath is forming round its cliffs. The end of the ridge, where it drops to the sea, goes by the somewhat irreverent name of Maclean's Nose.

The hill at the end of the peninsula is Beinn-na-Seilg, the ascent of which is the indispensable expedition from Kilchoan. It is the most westerly hill exceeding 1,000 feet in height on the mainland of Scotland. It is a short walk of a few hours up and down, but should not be hurried, as the summit is a glorious spot in which to loiter away the hours. Though only 1,123 feet above the sea it is a real mountain, with fine rock scenery and a real mountain view. The rock of which it is composed is the same volcanic gabbro which forms the splendid mountain architecture of the Cuillin in Skye, and though our little mountain is on a much smaller scale, and lacks the fantastic pinnacles of the Skye hills, it has bold rocks, and the northern lower peak ends in a fine precipice, which the *Mountaineering Club Guide* suggests might provide numerous interesting, if short, climbs. The ascent of the main peak is quite easy, and there can be few hills of such absorbing interest which can be climbed with so little exertion. If Ben Resipol has been described as the mountain for the middle-aged, Beinn-na-Seilg may fairly be reserved for one's old age! One member of our party actually made the ascent carrying an umbrella, which proved a useful protection while we sat through a heavy shower on the top. The dull rainy weather was a disappointment, as we could just see enough to appreciate what a wonderful viewpoint we had reached, but after we had waited some time a little light began to show through breaks in the cloud, and before coming down we were able to secure some photographs which, if not as brilliant as they might have been, yet give some slight indication of what the view ought to look like. Plate 102 is taken from the top, and shows the lower peak in the middle distance. This is a delightful little rock castle with the precipice on the farther side. Beyond this are other rocky hills, and the sea with the faint outlines of the shapely mountains of Rum rising above the long low-lying isle of Muck, and the end of Eigg on the extreme right. On a clearer day Skye also should be visible in the extreme distance. In the other direction the chief features are the views of Mull across the water.

The other chief expedition from Kilchoan is the walk to the Point of Ardnamurchan. There is a rough road all the way, and the distance is about five and a half miles. It may be varied by taking another rough road to Plocaig, a little village some three or four miles to the north, and then following the coast to the lighthouse. To go one way and return the other makes a pleasant round, and if you are lucky enough to meet the lighthouse-keeper's wife and persuade her to give you a cup of tea, as we did, this helps to fortify you for the tramp back over the less interesting bits of the inland road.

The coast scenery all round the point is bold and interesting. The cliffs as a rule do not rise sheer out of the sea to any great height, but finely shaped hills rise here and there quite close to the shore, and there are rocky promontories and little sandy bays which make every step of the way interesting. At Sanna Bay there is a spot which would make the fortune of a watering-place if it were less inaccessible. Reefs of rock jut out into the bay, enclosing charming little coves, floored with shining white sand composed almost entirely of crushed shells, and forming enticing bathing pools. Behind there is a tract of short grass and sand-dunes which would make a natural golf course, and at the back are steep gabbro hills enclosing a little gorge, which might prove an excellent practice-ground for rock scramblers. Someone, with more good taste than we often see in these days, has built an attractive residence here. Its low walls are built round a square court, and it is roofed with thatch, and it thus harmonizes admirably with the landscape, instead of clashing with its surroundings as so many of our seaside bungalows do.

Unfortunately our stay at Kilchoan had to be cut short, as the hotel was booked up for a cattle sale, and we were not able to do full justice in the few days at our disposal to this interesting region. Ben Hiant certainly deserves a visit, for the view from it must be grand, and there is a good deal more coast scenery to be explored than we had opportunity of seeing. This region is also interesting geologically. A few miles north of Kilchoan, we are told, is the site of the last active volcano in Britain. The erosion which has taken place in the countless ages since its activities ceased makes it difficult for the non-expert to pick out the actual site of the crater, but the flat valley bottoms, sometimes occupied by lochans and ringed round with bare gabbro hills, the smooth whale-back rocks familiar to visitors to Skye, and the bands and reefs of igneous rock, are evident signs of the volcanic action which has shaped this wild region.

I N   S O M E   W A Y S   T H E   M O S T
characteristic scenery of the Western Highlands is to be found in that part
of the coast lying opposite the islands of Eigg, Rum, and Skye. Nowhere
else is the sea so inextricably mixed up with the land, and nowhere else do
mountain, sky, and ocean combine in the same way to produce that infinite
variety of form and colour which we associate with this terrestrial paradise.

Arms of the sea wind for miles among the hills, and narrow channels open
out round unexpected corners where there was apparently no way through.
In every mountain view there is that expanse of water which we have again
and again pointed out to be one of the chief features required to complete
the perfect mountain landscape.

From its formation, divided up by long fiords many miles round, it is
not an easy district to explore without a yacht, and, even then, I always
maintain that the best views are seldom obtained from the surface of the
water. The photographer must have room to wander about on dry land in
order to select the best foreground, and he will usually find that there will
be a tendency to dwarf the mountains in his pictures unless he can climb,
even a little, above the level of the sea.[1]

The ideal solution perhaps would be to use the yacht merely as a movable
hotel, taking it from place to place to serve as a base of operations from
which walks and scrambles up the cliffs and over the hills could be made at
leisure.

For those, however, whose more modest purse will not run to such
luxurious methods there are two means of access available: by the West
Highland Railway to Mallaig and by the line from Inverness through Dingwall to Kyle of Loch Alsh. Boats connect some of the chief places, but they
are small and infrequent, except at the height of the season, which is not
usually the best time for a visit to these parts. The most useful service is
the steamer which runs from Mallaig to Kyle and Portree.

The West Highland extension from Fort William to Mallaig first crosses
the canal and then skirts the shores of Loch Eil. Farther on a glimpse is
obtained of Loch Shiel, a long, narrow fresh-water lake set deep among the
surrounding hills.

The voyage down this loch is a pleasant one, and the little inn at Acharacle
at the other end is a convenient headquarters for exploring the surrounding
country, as already described in Chapter IV.

[1] Will there be possibilities about an amphibious jeep?

The sea is first reached again at Loch Ailort, which bends round so sharply towards its entrance that it is difficult to believe that it is not completely landlocked. The line then threads its way among wooded hills, with occasional views of the sea, and it is worth while to leave the train for a few hours at Glen Beasdale halt in order to explore the interesting coast scenery of Loch nan Uamh.

The shore is very rocky, with little wooded islets here and there and numerous promontories jutting out into the water, the whole making an admirable foreground for the ever-changing pageant of the sky, as cloud and sunshine chase one another in endless succession over the confused jumble of sea and land (103). A range of mountains over 2,800 feet high form a fitting background towards the south-east, but I will not trouble the reader with their names, which are not easy to remember or spell.

Farther on we come to Arisaig, with its useful hotel, situated on an island-studded bay, with a fine view of the wonderful outline of the mountainous island of Rum. The latter must be well worth a visit, but is said to be so closely preserved that it is very difficult for a stranger to effect a landing.

Mallaig, at the end of the railway, is a convenient place from which to see the entrance to Loch Nevis, but the most attractive place to stop at on this part of the coast is Morar, on a beautiful little bay near the narrow strip of land separating Loch Morar from the sea. I have found few places so well placed for watching the glories of the sunset as this. In the early spring the sun goes down behind the splendid peaks of Rum, and all the colours of the heavens are reflected in the waters of the bay, which are beautifully framed by the rocky headlands on each side (105). When sunset and dinner coincided, our table manners were apt to deteriorate, for it became necessary to rush out with a camera between the courses to secure some special effect from the edge of the cliff.

It is extraordinary what an infinite variety of pictures can be obtained from almost the same spot under different conditions of weather and lighting. I have shown four examples here taken from within a few hundred yards of this hotel at Morar, all looking more or less in the same direction (104, 105, 106, 107), but I could easily double or treble the number if space permitted, each one being quite different from the rest. Most of them were taken either at or a little before sunset (105), showing the sun sinking into a bank of cloud in the late afternoon, and lighting up a path of glory across the waters of the bay. The end of the island of Eigg is seen to the left of Rum, just behind the nearer headland, which is part of the mainland; (106) was taken in changeable weather, with slight showers passing between the spectator and the setting sun, the outline of Rum being but faintly seen through the intervening mists. In (104) the sun is lower, a narrow bar of thick cloud making it possible to secure the photograph, while in (107) the sun is disappearing behind the low line of cloud along the horizon, and lighting up with a glow of colour—which the camera must perforce leave to the imagination—the layers of glowing mist reflected in the glassy sea.

Page 46

Besides the beautiful coast walks from Morar there are some very fine expeditions inland. The most obvious one is the track along the north shore of Loch Morar. This is a fresh-water lake about twelve miles long; it is also of considerable interest to the geologist as it is over 1,000 feet deep—deeper, in fact, than the sea for 150 miles out into the Atlantic beyond St. Kilda. This is all the more remarkable as the loch is separated from the Sound of Sleat by only a narrow isthmus about half a mile wide, intersected by a beautiful little salmon river emptying the surplus waters of the lake into the ocean by a series of rapids.[1] There is a group of wooded islands at the lower and broader end of the loch, but the quality of the scenery steadily improves as the head is approached.

An excellent view of it can be obtained from the hills about half-way along (108). This narrow loch is hemmed in on both sides by steep mountains, and the whole scene gives very much the impression of a Norwegian fiord.

About eight miles along the loch there is a narrow pass, between steep crags, leading through to Loch Nevis, one of the finest sea lochs along even this lovely bit of coast. Good walkers, who do not mind a tramp of twenty-two miles out and home again, may go through this pass, and, turning to the right, follow the shore for two miles as far as the rocks commanding the narrows dividing the upper and almost landlocked basin of Loch Nevis from the wider lower portion. From this point the view is very striking.

Most of the hills between the two lochs command fine views of both, and those who do not want such a long walk as that through the pass can thread their way through the bogs, and among the little tarns scattered about the rocky hollows, to the edge of the hills overlooking Loch Nevis. From about here a splendid idea can be had of upper Loch Nevis and of the grand mountain scenery round its head. The finest of these heights is Sgùrr-na-Ciche (3,410 feet), a shapely pyramid making an ideal culmination of the vista (109).

The entrance to Loch Nevis can also be explored by following the coast from Mallaig, the terminus of the railway, and climbing up and down the pathless hills, and in and out of the little rocky bays that line the shore. The views across the loch are of surpassing beauty, and rarely can the mixture of sea and mountain be seen to better advantage.

The view shown in (110) was taken looking across to Inverie Bay. The sharper peak under the big cloud rejoices in the name of Sgùrr Coire Choinnichean (2,612 feet), while the whiter and more distant mountain behind it is Ladhar Beinn (3,343 feet), which overlooks Loch Hourn. Seen in such weather as is indicated in this picture, with superb, towering cumuli sailing across the brilliant blue sky, with the sparkling sea below, the rich velvety hues of the dying heather softening the harshness of the rocks in the foreground, and a touch of unearthly beauty added by the gleaming snows of the distant hill-tops, Loch Nevis certainly seems to live up to its name, which, being interpreted, is the Lake of Heaven.

[1] Now being sacrificed to a local hydro-electric scheme.

The next great inlet to the north is Loch Hourn—the Lake of Hell. It is perhaps the finest of the great sea lochs and presents a great variety of scenery in its three great reaches. It is, however, very difficult of access and there are few places where any sleeping accommodation can be found within a reasonable distance of it. A small party might be able to find a room at Arnisdale or Kinlochourn, but there are no inns, and the approach would have to be made by boat from Mallaig or by rough roads from Tomdoun or Glenelg.

The Glenelg Hotel, where the visitor can now obtain better accommodation than that given to Dr. Johnson in his famous tour to the Hebrides, is situated near the sea overlooking Kyle Rhea, the narrow strait between the mainland and Skye, through which the tides rush with such force as to make navigation difficult. The water appears to come along in overlapping sheets, and the ferry boat has to work along under the lea of the shore some considerable distance above the opposite landing-place before it can edge its way gradually across the fierce current.

Glenelg and the ferry are reached by a road from Shiel Bridge at the head of Loch Duich. It rises rapidly with sharp zigzags to the pass called Mam Ratagan, a climb of over 1,000 feet from the water's edge. Hence there are superb views of Scour Ouran and the other peaks which surround the head of Loch Duich, but the Forestry Commission has planted the slopes with such masses of fir trees that they may tend to screen the view from the road as they grow up. If that happens it will be well to leave the car at the top for the engine to cool down and take a stroll along the hills on the right until a clear space can be found (111).

A rough but practicable road runs south from Glenelg to Arnisdale, enabling a visit to be made to the seaward reach of Loch Hourn. Here, again, we have a bone to pick with the Forestry Commission. A few years ago the slopes over the entrance to the loch were clothed with a fairy-like wood of native birches from which most entrancing views could be obtained of the fine sheet of water and the mountain ranges on the other side. Now, however, the birches have been ringed and slaughtered and the whole mountain-side planted with masses of conifers which will not only prevent access to the shore but will completely block the view from the road till it reaches the middle section of the loch. The Forestry Commission is, no doubt, engaged on work of great national importance, and in many places their young forests will be a valuable asset, but there are places from which they should be excluded, and this was one of them (113, 114).

As Arnisdale is approached there are some little islands near the shore, and the peaks of Ladhar Bheinn, Luinne Bheinn, and other distinctive hills come into view on the south side. Seen under favourable conditions the views along here may rank with anything in Scotland, especially in those wonderful moments when the weather is clearing up after a hail shower and the dark masses of vapour are being rolled back from the hill-tops by the breeze and are lit up by the sun emerging into the clear blue of heaven (112, 115). The road ends at Arnisdale, but a very attractive path winds along

115 Loch Hourn near Arnisdale—Clearing after Showers

M

117 Loch Carron from Plockton

118 Loch Torridon from North Shore

119 Skye from Loch Alsh

120 Skye from Loch Alsh

121 Loch Duich from Auchtertyre Hill

122 Loch Duich from Auchtertyre Hill—Snow Shower

123 Loch Duich from Totaig

125 Loch Duich and the Five Sisters

127　Loch Long (Ross-shire)

178   Ben Alligin from Loch Torridon

129 Loch Torridon and Ben Alligin

130   Pictish Fort—Loch Alsh

131   Pictish Fort—Glenelg

132 Loch Arkaig

133 Loch Garry

135 Loch Quoich—Reflections

137 Loch Quoich and Sgùrr-na-Ciche

139 Loch Quoich from South Shore

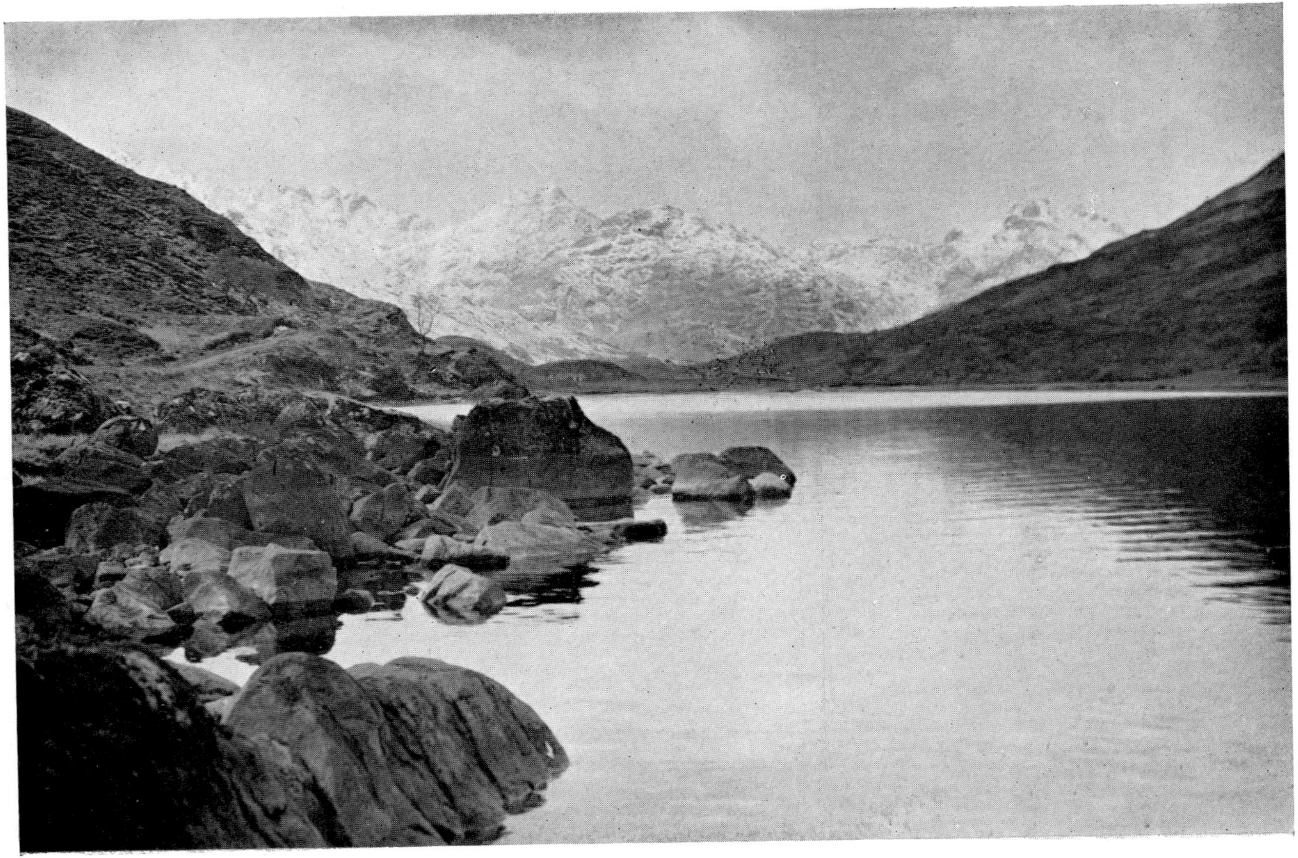

140 Loch Quoich and Rough Bounds

the shore among the rocks (116), and can be followed as far as the entrance to the narrow upper reach of Loch Hourn, which winds far into the heart of the hills. This, however, is better explored from the other side, and is best approached from Kinlochourn by the road from Tomdoun and Loch Quoich, which can be better treated in a separate section dealing with Knoydart and the hinterland of the great sea lochs.

Glenelg is the base from which to attack Ben Sgriol (or Screel), which stands like a sentinel over the north entrance to Loch Hourn, and whose pointed summit is a prominent feature from the sea and from the southern part of Skye. On the way to it, two or three miles from Glenelg, are some remarkable Pictish towers, one of which has preserved its full height on one side (131). As Ben Sgriol (3,196 feet) overtops its immediate neighbours and commands an extensive view of sea and land, with Skye on one side and a fine group of mountains on the other, it may claim to be the belvedere of the district, but I am unable to illustrate this as the weather was too hazy on the occasion of my visit for effective photography. As we were sitting on the summit what sounded like a sudden gust of wind disturbed the calm air, and on looking round we saw that a great golden eagle had flown close by us.

Loch Duich is the next great inlet, and ranks with the others in the grandeur of its scenery. The range of mountains called the Five Sisters of Kintail, of which the highest and central peak of Scour Ouran reaches a height of 3,505 feet, form the most perfect group to close the vista at the head of a loch to be found in Scotland. The road approaches by Glen Garry or Glen Moriston will be dealt with in another chapter, but the usual route to the west is by the Highland Railway from Inverness, via Dingwall to Kyle of Loch Alsh. The last part of the journey, especially along the beautifully wooded loch at Achnashellach, and along the shores of Loch Carron, is particularly attractive; so that anyone stopping in the neighbourhood should not be satisfied with the hurried glimpses from the train, but should at least explore the coast about the attractive village of Plockton.

Strome Ferry was the original terminus of the railway, but since the line has been continued beyond this place it has fallen into decay. Crags of no great height, but of striking shape, jut out into the water, which is here confined in a deep and narrow channel; but this channel opens out again into a broad sheet of water towards the head. The scenery here is of a quieter character than that of the neighbouring lochs, as the mountains do not rise so sheer out of the water, but the broader expanse of country, with the snowy tops of many distant mountains appearing over the varied outlines of the hills along the shore, is very pleasing, and gives this loch a character all its own. It is especially pretty here on a showery day, with the cloud shadows drifting over the wide expanse of hillside, and occasional hail showers to give contrast to the sunshine beyond.

From Strome Ferry the road to Plockton runs beneath a magnificent range of crags, and then passes through the thick woods of the Duncraig estate, which, before the War at any rate, gave a richness to the landscape rare in this wild country.[1]

N*

[1] This road has now been closed.

Plockton itself is pleasantly situated on a little harbour commanding a good view of the crags, and it is worth while to go out behind the village on to the little rocky promontories overlooking the loch. The surface of the sea is here broken up by numerous rocky islands and low reefs, which provide excellent foregrounds for the artist or photographer (117). Farther on the Applecross Mountains stand up well, while, in the far west, the wonderful outlines of the Skye hills add constant interest to the scene.

Kyle itself, the starting-point for Skye, is pleasantly situated on the straits, and has a comfortable little hotel owned by the railway company. The road to Balmacara goes inland, but there is a very pleasant walk along the cliffs overlooking Loch Alsh (119). In early spring, with snow low down on the hills and heavy storms raging inland, the view across these narrow waters can be exquisitely beautiful, though at times furious blasts of icy wind may make it difficult to enjoy the scene from an unsheltered position.

Fine views of sea and land can also be obtained from the hills on the farther side of Loch Alsh, near the entrance to Loch Duich (120). Our illustration was taken in stormy weather with bright intervals, and looking towards Skye. The narrows at the Kyle are well seen on the right, and the narrow, tide-swept channel of Kyle Rhea runs between the nearer slopes and the high hills above Kyle Akin, whose summits are just kissed by the storm cloud. The characteristic outline of the Broadford red hills and the jagged crests of the Cuillin are lost in a heavy shower sweeping across the island.

It is in weather like this that it is good to be beside the sea, with a wide expanse of water and broken mountain outline beyond. From such a spot nature can best be studied in all its various moods, as sun and shadow, calm and storm, follow one another in a quick and ever-changing succession of noble effects, never alike for more than a few minutes together. On the west coast there are many days like this—days hopeless for mountaineering on the big peaks inland, but by the sea always presenting something to watch and something to admire.

There is a good hotel at Balmacara for Loch Alsh, but the smaller one at Aird Ferry, by the Dornie ferry across Loch Long, is the best centre for all this district, now that the Shiel Inn at the head of Loch Duich has been closed.[1]

The best walk from Balmacara is up Auchtertyre Hill (1,481 feet), which has a surprisingly fine view of Loch Duich and the stately mountains round its head (121). A wooded headland divides Loch Alsh from Loch Duich proper, and the vista is closed by the fine range of the Kintail Forest, known as the Five Sisters, with the shapely peak of Scour Ouran (Sgùrr Fhuaran, 3,505 feet) towering up in the middle. This group makes an almost ideal finish to the view, and gives Loch Duich a claim to be reckoned among the very best of all Scottish lochs.

The whole composition of land, water, and mountain from this hill is so

[1] This ferry has now been replaced by a bridge. Visitors can now find accommodation at Kintail Lodge on the property recently acquired by the National Trust (see p. 7).

fine that I am tempted to give another photograph from almost the same spot, but taken under different conditions, when a sharp little snowstorm was passing over, from which Scour Ouran was just emerging (122). On the extreme left the white houses of the village of Dornie can be seen, with the Aird Ferry Hotel standing out in front of them, separated by the narrow channel which forms the entrance to Loch Long. The view of Loch Alsh, shown in (120), was taken from the top of the headland in the middle distance in front of the snowstorm.

We spent a very pleasant week at Aird Ferry. The weather was broken and stormy—so much so that we attempted only one real mountain walk, and had no opportunity of testing the steepness of Scour Ouran's formidable-looking slopes. It was, however, just right from a photographic point of view, and we had many beautiful low-level walks along the shores of the loch, and the hillsides overlooking them.

We were kept indoors for only two half-days by a continuous deluge, and then, when the rain stopped for a little while, there were grand effects to watch as the heavy clouds drove over the mountains, with here and there a little gleam of watery sunshine lighting up the ripples on the water, and emphasizing the blackness of the clouds around.[1]

It is quite good sport on these occasions to sally forth between the showers with mackintosh and camera, and find some suitable spot beside the sea from which to hunt the cloud effects whenever a suitable opportunity presents itself. But a good deal of patience is required for the game, as the light required shifts from one part of the picture to another, at one moment dazzling the eyes with the reflected glare from the backs of the waves, at another casting a gloom over the foreground that obliterates all detail, till one begins to despair of ever getting the right combination that will give a range of tones for reproduction within the power of the camera.

It is interesting, too, to see what very different effects can be got from the same spot, as I pointed out when describing the sunsets from Morar, and I have often secured half a dozen or more photographs from the same stand-point which were so different from one another that it is hard to believe they were taken at the same place.

A ferry-boat between Aird Ferry and Dornie has now been replaced by a bridge, but a longer crossing to Totaig on the opposite side of the entrance to Loch Duich is usually made by a motor-boat. The ferryman is summoned by a battered horn hanging up by the pier, which makes a noise like a cow in extreme agony, so that, if you are coming from the more distant shore, it is as well to give the ferryman notice when to look out for you, lest he should mistake you for an animal in distress and leave you stranded on an inhospitable shore miles away from anywhere.

The walk right round Loch Duich is strongly to be recommended. The prettiest bits perhaps are at Totaig and approaching the head, but the whole walk is fine. Totaig is situated at the tip of the headland, shown in (121) and (122), dividing Loch Alsh from Loch Duich. It is beautifully wooded, and

[1] See also (6).

little rocky bays and headlands, crowned with trees, make a perfect setting for the splendid group of snow-capped peaks at the head of the loch (123).

The view shown in (124) well illustrates the remarks made in the Introduction, where I spoke of the necessity of always having the camera ready for some unexpected effect which might be more beautiful than the view one had walked miles to see. I was just packing up in a heavy shower when the rain slackened and a sharp edge of black cloud formed an arch across the loch, under which the sun could be seen shining on a snowy peak in the distance. The effect was indescribably lovely as we gazed out of the gloom and rain towards the heavenly light beyond. This glimpse was quite unexpected, and lasted only for a minute or two, giving no time to select a foreground. I do not know how far the photograph will appeal to others, but to me at any rate, it recalls a beautiful effect in a way that no written description in a diary could do, and shows the necessity of being ready to seize the opportunity when it comes.

It is also worth while to climb the tree-clad hill above Totaig, which commands grand views in both directions. The walk in the other direction along the cliffs overlooking Loch Alsh, already referred to for its views towards Skye (120), is worth following as far as time and energy permit. Here there is the ruin of one of those very ancient Pictish forts, of which better preserved examples may be found near Glenelg (130, 131).

The mountains grow in size and importance as the head of the loch is reached, and the Five Sisters with Scour Ouran in the centre are most impressive, even when there is not much snow about, as shown in (125), which was taken a few days before the fall that whitened the peaks for the photographs shown in (123, 124). The return journey can be made along the north side of the loch to Dornie, and every step of the way is interesting, especially some beautiful parkland a few miles from the head of the loch (126), and from a spot a mile or two from Dornie, where the road climbs to a considerable height above the water.

Just at the entrance to Loch Duich there was a ruined castle, perched on a rock, and surrounded by the sea at high tide. This has been repaired, and occupies a commanding position at the entrance to the loch where, in the bad old days, the original owners probably used it as a point of vantage from which to prey upon any unarmed traders happening to pass that way.

The Kintail Estate at the head of Loch Duich has now been acquired by the National Trust for Scotland, as mentioned in our Introduction (p. 7). It includes the Five Sisters, Ben Attow, and neighbouring heights, and the public now has access to these grand mountains at all times of the year without interference from gamekeepers or deer-stalkers.

There is another pleasant walk to be had by the side of Loch Long, which must not be confused with the better-known loch of the same name farther south. It is five or six miles long, and very narrow, winding among the hills like a river. It opens out a little towards the head (127), displaying a good view of Ben Killilan (2,466 feet) and Sgùman Coinntich (2,881 feet), but is best seen when the tide is not too low, as the receding water exposes a mile of mudflats at the extreme end.

Sgùman Coinntich is particularly well placed for a view of sea and land, as already pointed out in our Introduction (see p. 10 and Plates 4 and 5). The ascent is rendered easy by a good path from the head of the loch.

The valley bends round to the right beyond the wooded crag seen in (127). There are good walks to the Falls of Glomach, and, eventually, to Glen Cannich or Glen Affric, but these are very long, even if a lift be obtained as far as the end of the road at Killilan.

The Falls of Glomach are the highest in Scotland, and have been acquired by the Scottish National Trust. They are, however, rather inaccessible, and are perhaps more easily reached from the shores of Loch Duich, on the other side.

Going farther north the next deep inlet is Loch Torridon, which takes us to the border of the country to be described in the next chapter. It is surrounded by some of the wildest and grandest mountains in Scotland, but, like many of the best things in this part of the world, is very inaccessible. There is nowhere to stay except a small inn at Shieldaig, and much of the country round is deer forest.

The most practicable way of visiting it is to drive the ten miles or so from Kinlochewe and walk along the pleasant path overlooking the plantations on the south side as far as there is time before driving back. Right opposite rises the splendid peak of Beinn Alligin (3,232 feet), with finely shaped buttresses supporting it on either side (128 and 129). Farther on there are some pretty birchwoods, and Liathach (3,456 feet) becomes more prominent, though this grand mountain is less imposing from this side than any other. Beinn Damh (2,958 feet) on the south side looks as though it would command a very wide and beautiful view, and the whole of this region deserves more careful exploration than I have been able to give it.

The walk along the north shore of Loch Torridon is also very attractive, and there is a rough road practicable for cars for at any rate part of the way. The views across the water of Ben Damh and the group of mountains between Torridon and Strathcarron are particularly fine, as most of them stand up boldly and present a very varied skyline (118). From Inver Alligin the walk could be continued to the hills overlooking outer Loch Torridon beyond the narrows dividing it into two parts, and very powerful walkers might even prolong it right round the coast to Gairloch.

THE GREAT NATURAL FAULT CALLED the Great Glen, through which runs the Caledonian Canal, divides the Highlands into two parts, and the country to the west of it contains much of the finest and wildest scenery in our island. A series of long narrow glens branch off to the westward whose lower portions include the finest valley and river scenery, while the enclosing hills grow grander and grander as they approach the coastal ranges which separate them from the great sea lochs.

The first starting from Fort William along Loch Eil, through which the railway to Mallaig runs, has already been mentioned. The next branches off from Loch Lochy, the first of the string of lochs which occupy the long straight depression filled by the canal, and is almost filled by the long narrow Loch Arkaig, a fine sheet of water some twelve miles long with wooded shores backed by steep mountain ranges. At its head Glen Dessary leads to the passes to Loch Nevis: this would be a fine centre for exploring the surrounding hills if ever the country were opened up to the tourist, but at present it is mostly deer forest and no accommodation is available. The road along Loch Arkaig is a very rough one, but just practicable for a carefully driven car, and the views from it across the loch are delightful. The chief feature (132) towards the head is Sgùrr Thuilm (3,164 feet), and at the entrance in Glen Dessary a finely shaped peak called Streap (2,988 feet) comes into view. Those who wish to explore these little-known hills can reach them more easily from Glen Finnan on the south.

The next two glens going north are Glen Garry and Glen Moriston, through which run the roads which eventually unite at Cluanie and provide the one through route for wheeled vehicles to Skye and the opposite mainland. Of these the first is the most important for the tourist as it leads to much splendid country which, with the help of a car to cover the road distances, can be explored from the hotels of Tomdoun and Cluanie.[1]

The Glen Garry road branches off from Loch Oich at Invergarry, and in about three miles reaches the Falls of Garry where the waters of Loch Garry find an outlet through a narrow gorge whose turbulent waters, it is to be feared, may make the mouths to water of the vandals in charge of the new hydro-electric schemes. The loch extends for nearly five miles and is mostly fringed with native birch woods, backed by the sugar-loaf of Ben Tee

[1] The inn at Cluanie has now (1946) unfortunately been closed.

(2,956 feet). If ever this country falls into the clutches of the Forestry Commissioners it is to be hoped that they can be induced to spare a broad belt of this native woodland along the shore and for a little distance above the road (133).

Tomdoun is about three miles above the loch, and here the road divides, one branch continuing up the glen to Loch Quoich and Kinloch-Hourn, and the other climbing over the hills to Glen Loyne and Cluanie. The river broadens out at intervals into narrow lakelets, of which the most important is Loch Poulary, from which Gairich (3,015 feet), the end of a bold range of hills, stands up well, and is, indeed, the principal feature ahead all along the valley (134).

Loch Quoich is certainly one of the finest of the fresh-water lochs in Scotland (135 to 140). It lies between Gairich on the south and a mountain called Gleouraich (3,395 feet) on the north, on which there is a deer sanctuary, and the north shore for half-way along the loch is fringed by the woods and plantations of Glenquoich Lodge. Glen Quoich, which branches off northwards, has the reputation of being the wettest spot in the British Isles, and is at any rate a rival in this respect of Stye Head in the English Lake District, and the slopes of Crib Goch on Snowdon. The upper part of the loch is best seen where some little inlets cut through the woods to the road just before reaching the bridge over the stream from Glen Quoich, or from the shore beyond, easily reached by crossing a narrow stretch of not very wet bog. Here a number of ridges radiate from the head of the loch and a number of bold peaks cluster round, culminating in the shapely peak of Sgùrr-na-Ciche (3,410 feet), which looks so splendid from the upper waters of Loch Nevis (137). This region between Lochs Hourn, Nevis, and Quoich, is called Knoydart, and contains some of the wildest and grandest mountains on the mainland; it is sometimes referred to as the Rough Bounds (140), and if ever economic pressure puts an end to the deer forests, the shooting lodge at Kinloch-Hourn would make an ideal centre for walkers and climbers unless we are shortsighted enough to allow the hydro-electric engineers to destroy the charms of Loch Quoich. During the past few years two abominable schemes for developing water-power in this region were thrown out by Parliament. The plan was to raise the level of Loch Quoich by a huge dam and turn its wild beauty into the commonplace of a tame reservoir. The water was then to be diverted to a power station at Kinloch-Hourn, thus violating another beauty spot, and at the same time ruining the fishing in the Garry and destroying one of the few sources of revenue of the inhabitants. Even now the danger of such vandalism is great as these schemes can easily be revived under the powers of the Hydro-Electric Bill. All this country of Knoydart and Glen Garry should be preserved from spoliation as a potential national park when access and communications can be improved.[1] If Kintail were added to it to connect with Glen Affric and Glen Cannich, a superb stretch of country could be preserved including some of the wildest mountains, the loveliest river scenery and the shores of the great sea lochs—all

[1] See the Introduction, p. 7.

that is most characteristic of the best the Highlands have to show. It is wrong to argue that it is too remote; the roads which connect it with the main through route from Fort William to Inverness could easily be improved and extended, while communications by sea from Mallaig could be rapidly increased to meet any demand. We look forward to a great increase in the tourist industry as one of the best prospects for the Highlands, and if inexpensive inns on the lines of the Swiss mountain hotels were established in such places as Kinlochquoich, Glen Dessary, Kinloch-Hourn, Barrisdale, or Arnisdale on Loch Hourn, Shiel Bridge on Loch Duich, on the shores of Loch Affric, at Inverie, or at the head of Loch Nevis, we should lay the foundations of a wonderful tourist industry for those who prefer fresh air and exercise amid the glories of nature to the gregarious excitements of Blackpool or Margate. If, however, we allow nature to be tamed or disfigured by commercial exploitation we must bid farewell to these dreams of opening up to all men of goodwill those beauties which have hitherto been only available for the few wealthy men who could afford the luxuries of a deer forest, but whose numbers may probably be drastically reduced by the taxation necessitated by the colossal expense of war.

To return to our exploration from Kinlochquoich, which can at present be reached by car from Tomdoun by a rather rough and narrow road, good paths lead up the valley at the head, from which stalkers' paths branch in various directions. Neglect has in places allowed them to sink into the bog just where they are most wanted, but they are a great help in exploring this rough country. One runs through Glen Cosaidh to Glen Barrisdale on Loch Hourn, with fine views of Ladhar Bheinn ahead most of the way. Another leads eventually to the same place by Lochan-nam-Breac, a wild little lake with steep rocky shores set deep among grand mountains, which in a small way may almost be mentioned in the same breath as the famous Loch Coruisk in Skye. Luinne Bheinn (3,083 feet) stands up finely at the end, one of the savage hills of the Rough Bounds (141), and can be ascended from the pass by which this path makes its way down to Barrisdale. I cannot speak from experience, but the view from this mountain should be fine as it is a prominent feature from the Arnisdale district across Loch Hourn.

Besides delightful walks on both sides of Loch Quoich, those on the south side commanding fine views of Gleouraich and its neighbour Spidean Mialach (136), a number of ascents can be made from Kinlochquoich. Gairich (3,015 feet) can be climbed with a descent to the bridge at the foot of the loch for Glen Garry; Sgùrr Mòr (3,290 feet), which stands up well from the north side of the loch (138), and Sgùrr-na-Ciche (3,410 feet), the monarch of the district, can be climbed without difficulty, but in some ways the most interesting ascent is that of Ben Aden (2,905 feet), which is defended by rocky ramparts that look formidable until a near approach shows an easy way of circumventing them. From the top there is a good view back over Loch Quoich and in every direction there are the bare rugged rocks of the surrounding hills (143).

Another very interesting ascent in this district is that of Sgùrr-a'-Mhao-

141 Lochan-nam-Breac

142 The Rough Bounds

143 On Ben Aden

144　Loch Hourn from Sgurr-a'-Mhaoraich

145 Upper Loch Hourn and Ladhar Beinn

146 Upper Loch Hourn

147 Upper Loch Hourn

148 Creag-a'-Mhaim

149 Loch Quoich from Cluanie Ridge

150 Loch Maree—Rainbow

151 Loch Maree—A Wet Day

153   The Saddle

155 Glen Affric (Loch Beneveian)

156 Glen Affric, Loch Beinn-a'-Mheadhoin (Beneveian)

157 View from Mam Soul

158 View from Sgùrr-nan-Ceathreamhnan

159 Beinn Eighe

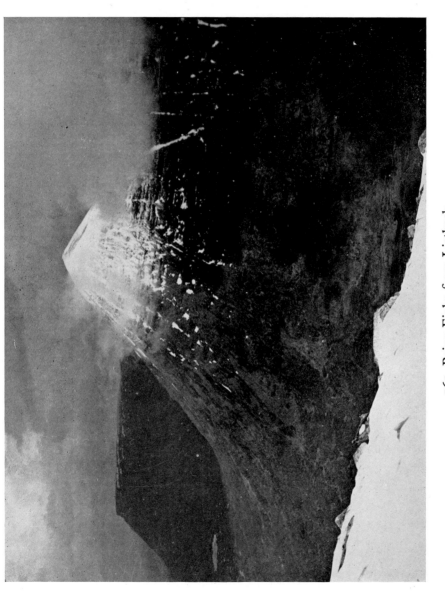

161   Beinn Eighe from Liathach

163   Liathach—Pinnacles

164 View from Sgùrr-nan-Ceathreamhnan

165 Beinn Eighe from Liathach

166 Beinn Eighe, Sgùrr Ban

167 Liathach from Beinn Eighe

raich (3,365 feet). A stalkers' path from near Quoich Bridge helps over the more tiring lower slopes to the spur called Bac-nam-Canaichean (2,111 feet), whence it is an interesting ridge walk to the summit. This commands a striking bird's-eye view of upper Loch Hourn backed by Ladhar-Bheinn (144) and Ben Sgriol, while in the other direction Loch Quoich and its surrounding mountains complete the picture. While we were enjoying the prospect some most beautiful furious-looking black clouds began to roll up from the east, causing us to return much more quickly than we had come up. As we reached the car at Quoich Bridge the deluge began, and we soon realized how Glen Quoich had gained its reputation for wetness, for we found the road behind us had been washed away and gave us some very bumpy crossings before we got back to Tomdoun.

A short run of five or six miles from Quoich Bridge leads through an interesting defile past a number of little lochans, to Kinloch-Hourn. The final descent is rough, steep, and serpentine, and nervous drivers or anyone not too confident in his brakes, should obey the notice at the top and leave his car there. At the head of the loch is a little dell shut in by steep mountains and tempered by the Gulf Stream which boasts such an equable climate that semi-tropical vegetation can flourish and things like eucalyptus trees can survive, and the hospitable farmhouse there can sometimes be induced to provide very welcome teas. The *pièce de résistance* here is the walk along the southern shore of the upper reach of Loch Hourn to Barrisdale, where it opens out to the middle reach. This is one of the most delightful walks in all Scotland; there is a good path, with very few soft patches, which runs now along the water's edge, now cut among the rocks on the side of a precipice, and now rising over a little pass to avoid a projecting cliff. Here and there magnificent spreading Scots pines, very different from the formal crowded specimens of modern commercial forestry, stand out among the crags, while ahead the sharply pointed buttresses of Ladhar Bheinn add majesty to the view, especially when storm-clouds sweeping over them part asunder to reveal their shapely peaks (145, 146, 147). Energetic walkers may vary their return by taking the path through Glen Barrisdale to Loch Quoich, or the still longer and steeper trudge over the shoulder of Luinne Bheinn and Lochan-nam-Breac.

From Tomdoun the road to Skye crosses a low pass before descending to Glen Loyne, a rather desolate valley, and then climbs to a height of over 1,400 feet before going down to Cluanie, whose small inn was a favourite resort of climbers and hill-walkers, as there are any number of interesting ascents to be made from this centre, and many of these ranges often retain much of their winter snow until late spring. The easiest of these expeditions is Creag-a'-Mhaim (3,102 feet), reached by a stalkers' path which starts from the top of the pass mentioned above, so that those who drive to this point have nearly half the climb done by the car. This is the end peak of the Cluanie Forest ridge which contains a series of no less than seven peaks exceeding 3,000 feet in height, all of which active mountaineers can traverse in one long day. Those who are less enterprising should at any rate

P

follow the ridge from Creag-a'-Mhaim over the first peak or two as far as Aonach-air-Chrith (3,342 feet), the highest of them, for the sake of the views (148, 149).

The hills to the north of the Cluanie Glen, between it and Loch Affric, are of considerable height, and mountaineers have a large selection from which to choose. The most prominent of them perhaps are Sgùrr-nan-Conbhairean (3,634 feet), A'Chralaig (3,673 feet), and the finely shaped Ciste Dhubh (3,218 feet). In late seasons these all carry a lot of snow and all command good and extensive views of the surrounding ranges.

The Five Sisters can also be climbed from this side, though Scour Ouran itself (3,505 feet) is best attacked from Shiel Bridge at the head of Loch Duich. The climb from sea-level to the top is mostly over grass and presents no difficulties, but it is probably one of the longest continuously steep slopes in the Highlands. The second peak of the group, Sgùrr-na-Ciste Dhubh (3,370 feet), not to be confused with its neighbour mentioned above, has some impressive crags and has splendid views not only across Loch Duich to Skye, but especially of the fine mountains across Glen Shiel, of which the Saddle (3,317 feet) is the most impressive (152, 153). This fine mountain possesses rock ridges bold enough to attract the climbing fraternity, on which ropes and ice-axes come in useful in wintry conditions. Its neighbours, Sgùrr-na-Sgine (3,098 feet), which stands up across upper Loch Hourn, and Faochag (3,010 feet), a fine sugar-loaf seen from Glen Shiel, are also worth attention (154).

The main road to the west from the Great Glen leaves Loch Ness at Invermoriston and joins the Glen Garry road at Cluanie. Passengers by this route can have their chance of looking out for the fabulous(?) monster, but Loch Ness itself, in spite of its length of twenty-four miles, is too straight to rank among the most beautiful of the Scottish lochs, and the hills lining the great trench are monotonous and lack character. Here the formal plantations of the Forestry Commission are more welcome than in the beauty-spots farther west. The River Moriston is a beautiful stream full of rocks and rapids and beautifully wooded, though the hills bounding the lower part of the glen are not of particular interest. Loch Cluanie is not impressive from the road, though it looks better from the water's edge on the south side, but it would suffer less than others if the level were raised. If, therefore, we have to sacrifice any of this country to the hydro-electric speculators let it be Loch Cluanie and Glen Loyne rather than Loch Quoich, and even the River Moriston rather than the Affric, Cannich, Farrar or Garry!

From Cluanie the combined road goes down Glen Shiel to Loch Duich, between the Five Sisters and the Saddle. These are too close above to be well seen, but Faochag (154) stands up well, beside the Saddle, and the narrow pass is almost a rival for Glencoe. At Shiel Bridge the roads divide, one going along the west side of Loch Duich with grand views backwards all the way, another climbs the Mam Ratagan for Glenelg, and a third follows the opposite shore to Dornie and the ferry over the narrow entrance to Loch Long, which has now been superseded by the long-projected bridge connecting it with the roads to Plockton and Kyle of Lochalsh for the crossing to Skye and the railway terminus. We have by this time reached the country described in our last chapter.

The next important break in the mountain barrier is larger and divides into three or four glens. It can be reached by a little side road from Drumnadrochit on Loch Ness, but is more naturally approached from Beauly on the sea coast a little west of Inverness. The main valley, called Strath Glass, splits up into three main glens, each running deep into the mountains, watered by a beautiful river and diversified by strings of lochs. The first, to the north, is Strath Farrar with Loch Monar and the fine peak of Sgurr-na-Lapaich as its principal features, the next is Glen Cannich containing Loch Mullardoch, and the third is Glen Affric. There used to be a through route to the west by a path from the end of Loch Affric over the passes between Ben Attow and the Five Sisters to Loch Duich, but it was a long tramp of thirty miles between the inn at Glen Cannich and that at Shiel Bridge, and since the closing of the latter the walk becomes a feat of endurance beyond the powers of most of us.[1]

The little Glen Affric Hotel at Invercannich, where Glen Cannich and Glen Affric meet, is the only base from which these valleys can be explored. There is a fair driving road as far as Affric Lodge, and a post car plies along it on certain days. The country is almost all deer forest, and has hitherto been rather jealously guarded during the season.

Glen Affric, and if possible its neighbours Glen Cannich and Strath Farrar, has been often put forward as suitable for inclusion in a national park. If this is to be carried out it is important that active steps in that direction should be taken without delay as its peculiar beauties are just those which would be most quickly destroyed by commercial exploitation. Although bounded by the highest mountains north of the canal, the mountains enclosing it tend to display rounded outlines, and when the snow has melted look more like exaggerated hills than real mountains, and cannot compete with the coastal ranges in outline or true mountain character, though interest increases as we reach the head of the glen. Sgùrr-nam-Ceathreamhnan (Kerranan, 3,776 feet), which continues the Carn Eige range to the west, is a finer mountain than its bigger brothers, and stands up grandly when seen from the hills of Skye or such a belvedere as Sguman Cointich on Loch Long, as already mentioned in p. 10 and (4). It has some fine ridges which may require care in wintry conditions, but its chief difficulty is one of approach as it is so remote from any inhabited place that it is quite an expedition to get to the bottom (158, 164).

It is not, therefore, so much to its mountains that this district can claim to be given special protection. It owes its charm more to the foreground features, the lovely river tumbling over its rock-girt course, through little gorges, over little waterfalls, or dancing through rapids, everywhere clothed

---

[1] The new hotel opened by the National Trust of Scotland, at Kintail Lodge, does something to replace the old inn at Shiel Bridge, and is a fine centre from which to explore this grand country.

in naturally sown woods of birch and pine. Heather-clad hills and spreading woods untamed by human regimentation add to the perfect beauty of the scene. To raise the level of the lochs by dams would ruin the beauty of the shores, and to interfere with the mountain torrents by depriving them of much of their water would be an act of wicked vandalism. Even the creation of a National Forestry Park would be a crime, because it would mean the destruction of so much lovely wild woodland, and if new plantations are ever to be introduced they should be kept well in the background, away from road, river, or loch. To destroy the birches shown in our plates of Loch Beinn-a'-Mheadhoin (Beneveian, 155, 156), as has been done to those at the entrance to Loch Hourn (see p. 48) would be an unforgivable offence.

My first visit was made at the beginning of June, when the fresh spring leaves were at their brightest and patches of snow still remained on the highest hills to give them dignity and importance. The most beautiful view was one we discovered for ourselves on the low hills over the eastern end of Loch Beinn-a'-Mheadhoin, reached by a branch valley running into the main one from the south, two miles south-west of Invercannich. The shores of the loch, and lower portions of the hills, were thickly clothed with the old native forest, and the fresh young leaves of the birches, with the sun shining through them, made a striking contrast with the dark, blue-green foliage of the pines (155). Coming over the low hill, from the park-like valley below, we found ourselves in a veritable Garden of Eden, with fairy-like silver birches dotted about in the rich brown of the dead bracken, and the gleaming waters of the loch beyond, backed by ridge behind ridge of mountain, culminating in the peaks of Mam Soul (3,862 feet), and Carn Eige (3,877 feet), the highest summits north of the canal.

In (156) a glimpse of Loch Affric itself is just seen through the trees beyond the end of Loch Beinn-a'-Mheadhoin, and the sharp peak at the end of the vista in the extreme distance is Scour Ouran (3,505 feet), which looks so splendid from Loch Duich on the other side. To the right of it the long ridge is Ben Attow (3,383 feet), a mountain which has obtained an extraordinary and undeserved notoriety owing to a strange confusion on the part of some ancient cartographer, through whose enterprise it has found its way into the geography books as the only mountain worth mentioning north of Ben Nevis. And this to the exclusion of many far finer, higher and more prominent peaks! To increase the confusion the ordnance surveyors have altered the name of the mountain to Beinn Fhada—apparently in an attempt to revenge themselves on their predecessors by causing the famous Ben Attow to disappear altogether, for it needs considerable faith to believe that both versions are merely attempts by different methods to reproduce phonetically the same name.

By driving as far as Affric Lodge we were able to see the greater part of Loch Affric, and to make the ascent of Mam Soul (O.S., Mam Sodhail, 3,862 feet). A stalkers' path made the walk quite an easy one after the wilder peaks farther north, but the distance from our base did not allow us to push on to Carn Eige, and by so doing add the highest peak north of the canal to our bag.

The view from Mam Soul was most extensive, for we looked right across Scotland from sea to sea, and, though it was June, great snow cornices still marked the edges of the ridges, one of which dipped far enough into a hollow to give us an opportunity for quite a good little glissade (157). In this picture the big, black hill near at hand, and on the right, is Sgùrr-nan-Ceathreamhnan (3,771 feet), the end peak of the range we were on; the faint, triple-headed mountain peering over its shoulder in the distance is Ben Sgriol (3,196 feet) over Loch Hourn, and the prominent peak in the middle is Scour Ouran, appearing over the long ridge of Ben Attow.

VII

The Wilds of Ross and Sutherland

T HE STRETCH OF COUNTRY BETWEEN
Loch Torridon and Loch Assynt contains the wildest scenery and grandest
mountains on the mainland of Scotland. Nowhere else are the outlines so
striking or the slopes so steep.

The district is not very easy of access, as the railways merely skirt its
fringe, and the roads are few and poor. Motor-omnibus services, however,
have been instituted, connecting the railways with three or four of the best
resorts, and these make it possible to get some notion of the character of the
country.

The best centres are Kinlochewe, for Loch Maree and the splendid
mountains round its head; Dundonnell for the wild Teallach range, and
Lochinver for the strange, isolated peaks of the Sutherland coast and walks
along the rocky shores. Accommodation may also be found at the Loch
Maree Hotel, at Inchnadamph on Loch Assynt, and at Gairloch, Poolewe,
and Ullapool, the last three being on the coast, and rather away from the
mountains.

There are some advantages in starting a holiday at the end of a spell of
bad weather. It is more interesting to have the beauties of a place gradually
revealed than to have them burst upon one all at once, and the clearing-up
effects after a storm are often the finest of all.

We arrived at Kinlochewe in the rain, with low clouds hiding everything
of interest, but, in the morning, these gradually lifted, revealing the whole
of the upper half of Beinn Eighe (Ben Eay) gleaming in a mantle of fresh
fallen snow, and as the sun reached it before the mists over the valley had
dispersed it seemed to hover over the dark foothills like some Himalayan
giant. Looking at it under these conditions we began to have considerable
misgivings as to our ability ever to reach those lofty ridges.

We spent the next few days exploring Loch Maree and the neighbouring
hills, keeping a sharp watch on the big mountain for any route promising
access to the ridge without too great difficulty or fatigue.

It was one of the attractions of this part of the world that there were no
satisfactory guide-books,[1] and though good maps were obtainable the new-
comer had something of the feelings of the explorer. Scotland has so far

[1] The lack of good guide-books to the hills has now been filled by the excellent series
published by the Scottish Mountaineering Club. Though these specialize chiefly on the
climbing routes, the ordinary means of access are usually also given.

proved too big a proposition for Mr. Baddeley, and the methods he has pursued with such success in the English Lakes or North Wales have broken down in dealing with so vast an area. In any case he has been able to describe only the regular tourist routes, and a few main roads, or a few selected peaks. The result was that one had to make out one's own route, choosing the gentlest slopes and avoiding the worst bogs, by the light of nature and experience, without any hints from outside. These conditions naturally lent a sense of adventure, reproducing in a mild form the sensations of the guideless climber, or of the early explorers making first ascents in the Alps.

This statement may of course sound absurd and exaggerated to the regular climber, and I do not wish to compare small things with great, but merely to suggest that this adventurous atmosphere may be sufficiently attained by the middle-aged pedestrian to add a special interest to his ramble, even if it does not involve the difficulties or excitements of the more ambitious enterprise.

Beinn Eighe is composed of seven or eight peaks joined by narrow ridges, the slopes of which are very steep, and composed largely of loose screes. These are very tiresome to walk upon, and, though it might be possible to crawl up almost anywhere, the ridge could be attained only by such an expenditure of energy that the pleasure of the scramble would be lost in labour and sorrow.

Careful observation, however, showed two weaknesses in the defences of the mountain. A little white peak, standing out in front of the main chain, appeared to be attainable by more moderate slopes than the rest of the ridges, and from it the upper part of the mountain could be reached by slopes which were steep in places, but not so long as to be altogether exhausting.

We tried this route a little later on, when the snow had melted to some extent, and found it practicable. The other and better way we discovered by accident. We had planned a walk to another and lower hill on the other side of the mountain, which looked as though it should command a good view of the northern precipices. When we reached the col between the two we found ourselves opposite a deep snow-filled corrie, at the head of which was a sloping gully leading right up to the top. We therefore dropped our original plan and attacked the bigger objective by this route, finding the deep snow covering all the tiresome, loose stones a great help in the ascent.

Once the ridge was attained it was easy to follow it in either direction, the only care necessary being to avoid treading too near the edge of the snow cornice lining the steeper side of the ridge.

Some of the peaks have fine and striking crags on the north side, which look very impressive when the gullies and slopes below are picked out by the snow (159).

The character of the mountain with its series of peaks is shown in the photographs (159, 160). In (160) the mountain beyond, whose outline from this point faintly suggests the Wetterhorn, is Liathach (3,456 feet), lone of the most striking peaks in this wild region.

There is not much difference in the height of the Beinn Eighe peaks; that of Sgùrr Ban (166) is given in the ordnance map as 3,188 feet, but the higher peak shown beyond, in which all the ridges meet, and which ought to be the real summit of the chain, does not appear to have been officially measured.[1] Actually the highest peak is the Ruadh-stac Mor (3,309 feet), which is a spur running north from the main ridge.

There is a grand view of Liathach from our nameless peak (167), enabling one to get a good impression of the wild and rugged character of this fine mountain. The slopes are everywhere exceedingly steep, and descend in a series of giant steps. It is possible to reach the top without serious climbing, but there are obstacles to be avoided on its long and pinnacled ridge (163), and inexperienced parties should exercise great care unless accompanied by someone who knows the way. The view of Beinn Eighe, and especially of Sail Mhor (3,217 feet), its second peak in height, is very effective (161, 165).

The corrie between the two highest peaks of Beinn Eighe, called Coire-Mhic-Fhearchair, contains a little tarn beneath the towering crags of the mountain, and is one of the wildest spots in this part of the world, and a rival of Loch Toll-an-Lochain under the Teallach (see p. 69). It can be reached by a rather long walk by a rough path through the bogs from Grudie Bridge on Loch Maree.

It is a pity that one of the grandest mountains in Scotland should be burdened with a name that can be spelt in any number of ways, and which no tongue can pronounce. I have adopted the spelling given in the ordnance map, but as the guide-books call it Liughach it is easy to see that there is considerable doubt as to what it should be, and I have not yet come across anyone bold enough to enlighten me as to the correct pronunciation.

A very good view of the north side of Liathach may be obtained from Beinn-a'-Chearcaill (2,376 feet), easily ascended from Grudie Bridge on Loch Maree. From this point it presents the appearance of a long serrated ridge culminating in a fine peak (162). The tremendous bluff of the western end is hidden behind Sail Mhor (3,217 feet), the end peak of Beinn Eighe, and marked by a striking snow-filled gully dropping half-way down the mountain in almost a straight line.

Beinn-a'-Chearcaill itself is a very remarkable hill, the summit being formed of an enormous rock plateau big enough to hold three or four tennis courts, and almost as level were it not for a few cracks and scattered boulders. The broken edge of this extraordinary formation forms the foreground of our picture.

Perhaps the most beautiful view of Laithach is that obtained from Loch Clair (168), an exquisite little lake with wooded shores just off the road from Kinlochewe to Torridon. The extraordinary western bluff is well shown, and the tent-like summit is a striking object when covered with its spring mantle of snow. It is even more impressive in gloom and storm with heavy thunder-clouds rolling up from the Atlantic and sweeping over the lofty ridges.

From the same little lake there is also a fine view of Beinn Eighe; our

[1] *The Scottish Mountaineering Club Guide* suggests a height of about 3,220 feet for this peak.

168 Liathach from Loch Clair

Q

170 Loch Maree

Mt. Brazeau Finch, from Cone'l'. Ridge

172   Loch Maree and Slioch

174 Ben Alligin from Beinn-an-Eoin

175　Slioch from Loch Maree

176 Gairloch

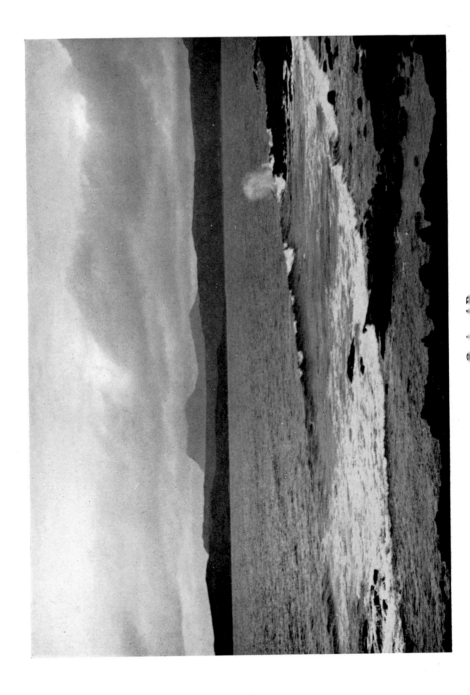

178 Little Loch Broom

Mt. Augusta. Head of the Yukon.

180 An Teallach, Sgùrr Fiona

182 An Teallach, view from Sail Liath

183 Coast near Ullapool

184 Loch Lurgainn and Stac Polly

186 Cul Mor from Loch Sionascaig

188 Quinag—View from Ridge

190 Kylesku—'thunder locally'

191 Loch Assynt and Quinag

192 Loch Assynt and Quinag

picture (169) is taken from just beyond, beside the channel connecting Loch Clair with another little lake called Loch Coulin. The upper part of Beinn Eighe is formed of white quartzite, and the broken screes look like snow even in summer, when the real snow is not there to emphasize the effect, as in our springtime photograph.

Though conveniently situated at the cross-roads Kinlochewe does not command any very striking prospect. It is, however, only a mile or two to the head of Loch Maree, and for the next four miles to Grudie Bridge the road skirts the edge of the loch, and every inch of the way is lovely.

The great feature of this end of the loch is the survival of the old original forest of Scots pine and silver birch, not planted in serried rows like a more modern plantation, but scattered over rock and hillside in picturesque confusion, allowing room for individual trees to develop their natural grace of outline.

The rocky shores of the loch add greatly to the picture, with little tree-crowned promontories jutting out into the water (170). The snowy peak in this photograph is Beinn Airidh Charr (2,593 feet), some seven or eight miles off down the loch.

From Grudie Bridge, which is surrounded by a fine group of pines, there is a glimpse up a wild valley to the highest peaks of Beinn Eighe (171), which were looking their best when this photograph was taken, as they glistened in the sunshine with a powdering of fresh-fallen snow.

Farther on the road runs a little away from the shore and the foreground is less beautiful, though Slioch (3,260 feet), which dominates the whole upper reach of the loch, towers up more grandly than ever over the surrounding hills (172). When the Loch Maree Hotel is reached the loch widens out and there are a number of islands; this is probably the most visited part of the loch, though, to my mind, the wooded upper reach is the finest part.

The hills at the foot of Loch Maree are well worth exploring, as they command wonderful views of the loch, studded with islands and backed by the stately mass of Slioch and the more distant ranges of Beinn Eighe and its neighbours (175). There is a great advantage in staying in a hotel beside the water, especially in bad weather. When long expeditions are prevented by cloud or rain there are often short intervals when the sun struggles through and produces fleeting effects best seen across the loch by those on the spot. To sally forth and enjoy such temporary breaks with a return to shelter when they are over helps to relieve the tedium of a wet spell when on holiday. I once spent a week or so at the Loch Maree Hotel under these conditions, and I never saw so many rainbows (150). Low clouds wrapping the lower slopes of the hills often make quite a good picture on a wet day (151). One of the few high expeditions we made that holiday was the ascent of Beinn-an-Eoin (2,801 feet), one of the hills which stand up in the background from Gairloch. We arrived at the top just in time to see a grand glimpse of Ben Alligin peering through the clouds (174); then the rain came on again and we had a very wet tramp home through the bogs.

Despite its formidable appearance from this side Slioch can be ascended

R*

easily from the back. Crossing the river at Kinlochewe the path along the opposite side of the loch leads to the entrance to Glen Bianasdail, a straight narrow cleft between the hills, with a fine tumbling stream, bringing the water down from the upland lake, Lochan Fada.

We started out with the avowed intention of exploring this lake, but when we reached the top of the pass it looked as though we should have to go a long way to get a different view, and big streams without bridges might provide unexpected obstacles. On the other hand the slope above looked inviting and tempted us upward. A short scramble led us up to a ridge which ran almost directly to the summit, giving a much easier route than we had expected.

There was a great deal of snow about, picking out the gullies, and giving the ridges quite an Alpine appearance. Though the weather was fine on the whole there was a curious sort of gloom in the distance, and a slight haze, which did not, however, hide the snowy tops of the mountains looming through it like ghosts.

The whole country between Slioch and An Teallach looks interesting, with its series of wild mountains and lochs, but the absence of paths and bridges, and the distance from any inhabited spot, render it very difficult to explore.

The ascent of Slioch just described is a good example of the right way to start for a walk in the Highlands. It is a mistake to take things too seriously, or to have too definite a plan in such an uncertain climate as that of the west coast. To be ready to seize an opportunity, or to vary one's objective according to the weather, is one of the secrets of a successful holiday.

I can never understand why all writers of books about the Highlands seem to choose the worst possible weather for their climbs. They invariably seem to get half lost in clouds; to be driven to attempt the most difficult and exhausting routes, and to see nothing when they get there. I suppose there is some pleasure to the man overflowing with animal strength and vigour in matching his powers against the rage of the elements; in fighting his way up rock face and ridge against roaring gale and driving rain, but I must confess that I like to see something when I have dragged myself up a steep slope, and as one gets older there is more need for economy of effort if one is to make the best of a mountain holiday. It is, of course, impossible to avoid being caught by a sudden change of weather now and then, but it is foolish to start off for the mountain-tops under obviously hopeless conditions, and one should have the strength of mind to turn back when the weather looks like breaking up.

The road along Loch Maree reaches the sea at Gairloch, where there is good accommodation and where extensive views can be obtained across the sea as far as the Outer Hebrides. Beinn-an-Eoin, Baosbheinn, and Ben Alligin also stand up grandly across the bay, and this is one of the spots where sea and mountain scenery can be combined (176). There are interesting walks and drives along the coast in either direction, that going northwards passing by Poolewe and Aultbea to Gruinard Bay (177) to Little Loch Broom and Dundonnell.

If I were asked to name the wildest and grandest mountain on the mainland of Scotland I should, perhaps, give the palm to An Teallach (The Challich). It can be visited from Dundonnell, where there is a comfortable little inn, but it is best to go early in the year as it is all deer forest, and strictly preserved in the season.

Dundonnell is reached from Garve station on the Highland Railway, whence a motor-omnibus runs to Ullapool, thirty-four miles distant. It is necessary to arrange for a trap to meet the omnibus about nineteen or twenty miles from Garve, where the road branches off from the Ullapool route, the distance from here being about fifteen miles.

Dundonnell is thus somewhat cut off from the world, but is well worth an even more tiresome journey. The greater part of the drive is over comparatively dull moorland, over 1,000 feet above the sea at the highest level, and only becomes really interesting when the descent to the Dundonnell valley begins. The last few miles are very pretty, with wooded slopes and rich pastures at the bottom, reminding one of the English Lakes more than is usual in Scotland.

A little below the road there is an extraordinary gorge, a narrow chasm some hundred feet deep, with the river rushing along at the bottom, and so narrow that a good jumper could almost clear it at a bound. It is half hidden in deep heather, and would be a dangerous trap to come across suddenly in the dark.

The inn is situated at the head of Little Loch Broom, a noble sheet of water walled in by steep hills. Though it cannot be classed as one of the finest of the sea lochs it has some good features, and, as it runs in a north-westerly direction, it looks best in the late afternoon when the sun is partially hidden by thick clouds, and is sending long rays through these, lighting up the water with a track of gold (178).

An Teallach itself is not seen well from the loch, as it is hidden by its lesser satellites. The chief feature is Sail Mhor (2,508 feet), a spur of the greater chain standing rather apart from the rest, with the top powdered with fresh snow as shown in our picture.

We made this hill the object of our first expedition, as it seemed the right spot for a bird's-eye view of the district from which to reconnoitre the Teallach on its northern and least precipitous side in the hope of finding a reasonable way up. There was an icy gale blowing on the top which spoilt some of the pleasure of the walk, but we had a glimpse down to Loch-na-Sheallag on the farther side, a little lake hemmed in by rugged mountains, which would be well worth a visit if it could be reached from any direction without an undue expenditure of energy.

We were also able to plan a method of attack on the highest peak of An Teallach, which we carried out successfully a day or two later. There is a flat-topped spur, a little over 2,000 feet high, running north from the main peak, which can be attained by a fairly steep scramble from the seashore. From this it is easy to reach the higher ridge from which the final peak rises. The last ascent is steep and laborious for anyone not in good training, but the view from the top is an ample reward for the effort involved.

Page 67

The ground-plan of the mountain is roughly in the shape of the letter E, of which the top stroke is the end of the ridge by which we ascended. The summit, Bidein a' Ghlas Thuill (3,483 feet), is just where the centre stroke reaches the upright one at the back, while the second peak, Sgùrr Fiona (3,474 feet), with its attendant pinnacles, forms the lower part of the upright stroke, and a fine craggy spur called Sail Liath forms the bottom of the letter.

At the back of An Teallach the slopes consist of exceedingly steep screes, but towards the inside of the E there are tremendous precipices of bare rock. Plate 179 shows the crags of Sgùrr Fiona from the highest summit.

We managed to scramble along the ridge to the sharp peak on the right of the picture, which is actually the highest part of Sgùrr Fiona, but time would not allow of an attempt upon the rest of the ridge to see whether a way could be found round the very formidable set of pinnacles beyond without involving anything in the way of serious rock-climbing. No finer mountain outline can be found in Scotland, outside the Cuillin Hills of Skye, than that presented here.

In order to explore the south-eastern, and finest, face of the mountain, with its precipices and deep corries, the road up the glen should be taken for about three miles from the hotel, till a track comes in from the south just beyond a tributary stream. This track should be followed for about a mile, when the stream should be crossed at the most favourable spot, and the ridge opposite mounted. This ridge is a very remarkable geological phenomenon: it runs in a straight line for about two and a half miles, rising from the bottom of the valley to a height of 1,400 or 1,500 feet at the upper end. About a quarter of the way up it is split through by a fault which provides a formidable obstacle to anyone desiring to follow the ridge. It should therefore be attacked from beyond this point. The ridge slopes up gently on the outside, but towards the mountain is broken off in a precipice, or descends in great steps to the hollow in which the stream flows, like a vast Greek theatre—an impression which is accentuated by the way in which it curves round at the top towards the mountain, and by the pure white colour of the rock of which it is composed. It is hard and slippery and the surface is mostly bare, with huge smooth slabs of shining rock, and pools of clear water in the hollows, which leave only room for little patches of heather in the cracks, especially near the edge. The whole forms a wonderful platform from which to watch the crags and pinnacles of An Teallach, especially in stormy weather when the clouds roll over the crags in cascades of mist, and peak and pinnacle appear now together, now alone, picked out from the encircling gloom in an ever-changing succession of noble pictures, and looking twice their real size in the uncertain light.

Our illustration (180) gives some notion of the broad white slabs of the 'Marble Ridge', as we christened it from our fancied comparison to the tiers of a Greek theatre.

I do not know what the rock really is, but an account of this district by a competent geologist[1] would be interesting and instructive. The great mass of the mountain seems to be composed of Torridon sandstone and gritstone, capped probably by patches of quartzite or other hard rock, like other hills in Ross, which have preserved the base beneath them from erosion and caused the towers and spires that give this mountain its unique character.

The hard Torridon sandstone is of a dark reddish colour, and seems to lie in a series of superimposed beds; these, when broken away sharply at the edges, form a series of parallel terraces or ledges which are picked out by the snow in the photograph.

Much the same formation occurs on Liathach, which we were examining a few pages back, and there the hard quartzite caps forming the peaks are clearly to be seen in summer photographs when their lighter colour is not disguised by snow.

Right under the crags of Sgùrr Fiona, in the hollow, is a little lakelet, almost surrounded by towering cliffs, with the bare rock dipping straight into the dark water. It is a striking scene, but it is difficult to do it justice in a photograph, for, in order to do so, it would be necessary to use such a wide-angled lens to include the tops of the crags that it would dwarf their apparent height.

The fine precipices on our left in the picture (180) are part of Sail Liath, the southernmost spur of the mountain, forming the bottom stroke of the letter E. This can be climbed without difficulty from the end, though the slope is steep and fatiguing in places. But it is well worth the effort, as it commands a very fine view of Sgùrr Fiona and the pinnacles from a fresh angle (181), and a most extensive panorama to the south and west.

The view up the long valley at our feet, with the river winding at the bottom, walled in by ridge behind ridge of wild mountains, was especially impressive (182). The prospect was closed in the distance by Beinn Eighe's long chain of peaks, and, a little nearer to the left, by our old friend Slioch, whose steep northern bluff is unmistakable.

Dundonnell seems very far from the rest of the world. The post comes via Ullapool, itself thirty-four miles by motor-omnibus from the railway; it has then to be ferried across Loch Broom, about three-quarters of a mile by boat, and thence it has to be carried on foot, or in a light cart, by a very steep and rough road for another six or seven miles over the mountains to Dundonnell.

After a pleasant stay at Dundonnell we decided to move our base of operations northwards, and explore the remarkable country on the borders of Ross and Sutherland.

The first stage was to reach Ullapool, where we spent the night, after an interesting afternoon examining the beauties of Loch Broom. It is a long inlet with a distant view at the head of the Fannich Mountains, whose fine

[1] The introductory volume of *The Scottish Mountaineering Club Guide-Book*, which has now been published, contains a brief and rather technical description of the geology of the Highlands, but details of any particular district could not be included in the space available.

outlines close the vista very satisfactorily. The east shore is clothed in dense plantations of fir-trees of many different kinds, giving it a softer look than is often found in this wild and desolate country, but the trees are so thick in places that, for miles on end, it is difficult to get a glimpse of the view from the road.[1]

It is a great contrast to the scene a few miles north of Ullapool, where there is a typical bit of west coast scenery just beyond the entrance to Loch Broom. Steep and rocky hills, clad in heather, dip into the sea, or send out long spits of sand or rock to divide one inlet from the next (183). Beyond the flat spit, with one or two lonely houses on it, is a rocky promontory, on the farther side of which is the entrance to Loch Broom, and beyond again, with its top wreathed in clouds, as in our picture, is Beinn Ghobhlach (2,082 feet), the highest peak on the tongue of land separating Loch Broom from Little Loch Broom.

Next morning we hired a car, intending to reach Inchnadamph on Loch Assynt, about twenty-four miles off by road, breaking the journey by a little detour to visit Loch Lurgainn.

This is the first of the extraordinary series of lochs which are dotted all over the western part of Sutherland, and in such numbers that the map seems to show almost as much water as land. Loch Lurgainn is rather a desolate sheet of water of irregular outline, but is surrounded by some of the most striking mountain shapes in Scotland. Ben More Coigach, no longer a long straight ridge of rock stretching out into the sea, as viewed from the Ullapool neighbourhood, is here seen in profile, supported by a cluster of sharp-peaked satellites. On the other side are Stac Polly and Cul Beag, the first of the extraordinary row of isolated peaks that give a special character to the scenery of this district. Stac Polly (184), though only 2,000 feet in height, is a particularly striking example of these. It rises steeply on all sides from quite low ground, and is crowned by a great comb of rocks, which gives it a distinctive outline from all sides.

With a little judicious planting to soften the austerity of the scene, this lake could be made one of the chief beauties of Scotland, for in few other places could such a striking and varied mountain outline be found as a background to any lake. If an unpretentious inn could be established on its shores, and reasonable access obtained to the neighbouring deer forests, there is no question that it would make a splendid holiday centre.

Good walks could be found in every direction; interesting mountains with fine views could be climbed, and the rocky sea-coast of Enard Bay is within easy reach. The numerous lochs and streams would be a paradise for fishermen, and Stac Polly, and probably also Cul Beag and Cul Mor, would provide entertainment for the rock-climber without too great an expenditure of energy in getting to the foot of his objectives.

Viewed from the heights at the farther or western end this loch forms the centre of an amphitheatre of hills presenting as varied and wild an outline as any in Scotland (185). Stac Polly, with its comb of rock, is easily

[1] Have these trees fallen victims to the demands of war?

identified on the left, Cul Beag is on the extreme right, and Cul Mor fills up the gap in the middle very satisfactorily.

Not far off there is a larger loch of irregular shape, with wooded islands, rocky headlands, and secluded bays. It is called Loch Sionascaig in the ordnance map, but Baddeley prefers the cacophonous version of Loch Skenaskink. Stac Polly, Cul Beag (2,523 feet), Cul Mor (2,786 feet), and the more distant Suilven (2,399 feet), each rising in isolated grandeur from the undulating heathery country round the loch, form a magnificent background.

Plate 186 shows Cul Mor from the north-western end of the loch, which is the least inaccessible part of it; but it would take a long time to exhaust the charms of the winding shores of this loch, especially in its present deserted condition, for it is without paths or bridges, and some distance from any road.

Loch Assynt is the largest fresh-water loch in this district, being seven or eight miles long, and can be best explored from Inchnadamph. Ben More Assynt (3,273 feet) and its spurs command the head of the loch, but the chief feature is the long irregular cliff of Quinag, with its series of peaks of from about 2,500 to 2,600 feet in height, well seen from the lower end (188, 191, 192).

A rough road strikes off a little beyond Inchnadamph, and, passing under the cliffs of Quinag, leads to Kylesku. This is a very beautiful spot at the junction of three sea lochs; it possesses a minute inn and a ferry, when one can find the ferryman. It would make an ideal centre for anyone fond of boating, as the scenery is fine and varied, but communications by land are difficult. This type of country is most impressive on an unsettled day, when hail and thunder showers are sweeping across the hills at the head of the lochs, while an occasional gleam of sunshine helps to emphasize the blackness of the storm (190).

The most repaying ascent in this district is of Quinag. Though the highest point is only 2,653 feet above the sea, it is a real mountain and its isolated position increases its importance. It is also one of the easiest and least fatiguing as the Kylesku road rises to over 800 feet before the climb begins, thus cutting off a third of the height to be scaled. Once the main ridge is attained it is a delightful stroll over the series of peaks and saddles which make up the mountain. Numerous lochs and the sea diversify the view, and on the occasion of my visit wisps of cloud sweeping in from the sea greatly increased the apparent height of Canisp, Suilven, and the neighbouring peaks (188). Fine precipices overhang the sea lochs at Kylesku.

After Quinag the most interesting ascent from Inchnadamph is that of Canisp, as the proximity to the aiguilles of its neighbour Suilven gives it a character all its own. After a spell of bad weather, during which snow fell even down to the valley, it suddenly cleared up, and we decided to attack our mountain by its southern ridge as we wanted to get Suilven more end on, while the snow was picking out the gullies (189). The tramp through the bogs and lower slopes was rather sloppy in the fast-melting snow, but going was better when we reached the higher ground. The view from the top is very extensive, with the sea glittering behind Suilven (206), and the brilliant sunshine on the fresh fallen snow seemed to fill the whole landscape with light and colour. To the north the snow-capped domes and ridges of Quinag rose grandly over Loch Assynt (207).

Lochinver is situated on the coast, about four or five miles from the foot of Loch Assynt. The hotel was originally built as a residence for the Duke of Sutherland and possesses spacious halls and imposing staircases, with the result that its charges are higher than those of most of the less palatial establishments referred to in these pages. However, it is well placed for exploring the fine coast, and is a possible, though rather distant, base for an attack on Suilven.

The low cliffs to the northward afford a good view of the strange series of isolated mountains already referred to (199), which, instead of being arranged in a connected chain, as almost everywhere else, seem to have been dropped down separately like specimens in a museum. Beginning on the left in our illustration we have Suilven, the most remarkable of them all, then Cul Mor, Cul Beag, and Stac Polly; Canisp and Quinag continue the series outside the picture on the left.

The coast to the south of Lochinver is very rocky, reminding one in places of Cornwall, were it not for the mountain background which gives an interest to the hinterland, which is lacking in its south-coast rival (198, 200). The background in our picture is formed by Stac Polly and the long ridge of Ben More Coigach.

The feature of all this neighbourhood is the extraordinary outline of Suilven—or the Sugar-loaf, as it is vulgarly called, owing to its appearance when seen end on. It is always popping up, like an enormous thimble, in unexpected places. From the side it is a double peak, shaped something like a dolphin, with a great rounded head, and a sharp pointed tail beyond a depression in the middle. From beyond the tail the mountain looks like a regular aiguille, if we may use an Alpine term (189, 194). It is inaccessible all round to any but expert climbers in good training, except just in the middle, on either side of the saddle separating the two peaks. Here there is a steep grassy gully up which it is just possible for the ordinary mortal to crawl, though not without some puffing and blowing. But once the ridge is gained the way to the higher summit is easy (206).

The view is chiefly remarkable for the vast number of lochs dotted all over the country below. These are of all shapes and sizes, and can be counted literally by the hundred. Truly Sutherland should be a paradise for the fisherman!

Those who wish to combine a sea and mountain holiday might do much worse than settle down at Achiltibuie on the coast between Lochinver and Ullapool. It is not likely to be a crowded or fashionable resort as it is some fifty-six miles from a railway station, thirty-four of which may be covered by motor-omnibus to Ullapool. Beyond this the road skirts the beautiful chain of lakes beginning with Loch Lurgainn, described above, and then bends round to the coast, past Loch Bad-a'-Ghaill, whence there is a striking

193 Suilven from Loch Borralan

194 Suilven 'Aiguille' from top

195 Cnoc-an-Freiceadain

196 Tongue Bay

197 Stac Polly from Loch Bad-a'-Ghaill

198 Clachtoll Bay

200 Coast near Lochinver

217. View from Pen Maen Crianak

202 View from Ben More Coigach

203   Achiltibuie—'West Coast Weather'

204 Sunset and Summer Isles

s

205 Enard Bay Cliffs

206 Suilven from Canisp

208 Ben Loyal

210   Loch Eriboll

all Piccard

212 Whiten Head from Rispond

214 Kyle of Tongue from Melness

215 Ben Hope and Loch Hope

216 Kyle of Durness

217 Arkle

218 Ben Stac

219 Sound of Raasay from Portree Cliffs

220 The Storr

221 The Old Man of Storr
222 Quiraing

glimpse of Stac Polly (197). On first arrival we were a little disappointed as the haze hid the beautiful view across the bay, and the immediate surroundings of the little inn, consisting mainly of forlorn-looking potato-fields and crofters' cottages were not inspiring. Further exploration, however, completely altered our impression. Directly we had crossed the potato-fields we came to a delightful little promontory with a fine rocky coast and splendid views across the sea as soon as the weather cleared. These may be still further improved by climbing Ben More Coigach (2,438 feet), which is so placed as to combine most of the conditions required for an ideal viewpoint. Situated just at a corner where the coast bends round at right angles, Ben More commands a wide stretch of sea dotted with islands, while to the west a series of long promontories jut out, separated by narrow inlets. On the land side these culminate in the grand Teallach Range, whose snow-covered tops are seen in our illustrations (201, 202) across a wide arm of the sea whose surface is dappled with cloud-shadows. To the south is Loch Broom, backed by the Fannich peaks, and a tangled mass of hills fading away into the distance, while to the east the crags of Ben More itself drop steeply towards the Lurgainn group of lakes with Stac Polly and the other shapely peaks around them.

The rocky coast opposite the Summer Isles is an excellent hunting-ground for the photographer of weather effects. Plate 203 was taken near here on a stormy day in an interval between the showers, and attempts to give some suggestion of the wild weather of these western coasts. Plate 204 was secured under calmer conditions with the sun sinking to rest behind the islands.

The continuation to the north-west of the Coigach peninsula is dull inland, but along the coasts, especially along the side overlooking Enard Bay, there is cliff scenery which would do credit to the best bits of the Cornish coast. Little sandy bays, jagged rocks and imposing cliffs keep up the interest all the way, while the strange outlines of Suilven and the Sutherland hills rising across the bay add a touch of mountain grandeur which can only be found on these western shores (205).

VIII

The Far North

T WENTY YEARS AGO I REFUSED TO take a motor-car on a Highland holiday, feeling that it would provide too great a temptation to stick to the roads and to reduce the call for the physical exercise which was one of the objects of a holiday. Increasing years, however, have caused me to modify this opinion. In the Highlands the distances to be covered are considerable, and a car, if used in the right way, helps to concentrate effort on the finest spots, without too great an expenditure of energy in getting to them. Inns and resting-places are often many miles apart, and if one is chosen as a centre the field available for exploration is enormously increased. A sudden break in the weather, which is all too common in these parts, is far less trying if the car is waiting at the bottom of the hill to run us back through the rain to our headquarters. But the car must be regarded as an adjunct to, and not a substitute for, our legs. The best scenery is usually on cross-country tracks or on the heights above, and though the road frequently leads through glorious country it is only those who are prepared to leave the car to find their own point of view that get the full benefit of the expedition. Do not, therefore, make the drive the main object of the day's trip, but use the car as a movable base of operations if you wish to make the best use of the opportunities it gives you. Nobody can appreciate beautiful scenery while being whirled through it at a great pace, and the driver must keep his attention fixed on the road ahead. Even the old and infirm, who are unable to scramble up to the hill-tops, should cause the car to stop from time to time at the best places, and if possible alight and stroll about to find the best setting and foreground for the view in front of them.

For those who use the car rightly, a trip to the far north has many attractions. The country is less concentrated than farther south, the mountains more isolated and distances between beauty-spots are greater, but the roads go through some very beautiful country, and there are many places, especially near the north coast, where quite a short stroll from the car will lead to cliff and beach scenery of a very high order. Those who can should, of course, climb the hills as usual, but the approaches to them are often a long way from any habitation so that the car comes in useful for them too. Much of this country is deer forest, and visitors should therefore time their holidays in such a way as to avoid unpleasantness on the part of gamekeepers.

The best approach is through Lairg, where the two chief roads divide, and

Page 74

a round trip can be made going by one and returning by the other. There is also an alternative route by Loch Assynt and the ferry at Kylesku, described on p. 70, for those who are prepared to risk the difficulties of bad roads and delays at the ferry. For those coming from Ullapool direction there is a connecting road to the Lairg route through Invershin, which commands fine views of the wild hills of the Ross and Sutherland border. The distant glimpse of Suilven from Loch Borralan, near the Altnacealgach Hotel, is particularly striking (193), and there must be many fine walks to the Cam Loch and the wild country between it and Loch Lurgainn.

Taking the easternmost road, the first part of the journey is not particularly exciting as it runs through featureless moorland, until Altnaharra is reached, where there is a fishing inn overlooking Loch Naver, and there are views across the loch to Ben Klibreck, which shares with Ben Hope the honour of being the only mountains to exceed 3,000 feet to the north of Loch Shin.

The next feature of interest is Loch Loyal, but as the road runs along the west shore between the water and Ben Loyal it is rather too near to the mountain to command impressive views, but in any case the finest side of the mountain faces the north-west on the other side. The easiest ascent is from about the middle of the loch by a ridge which rises after crossing a not very formidable little stretch of bog to lead towards the northernmost second highest peak (Sgor Chionasaid, 2,320 feet). Ben Loyal consists of a long ridge crowned by four or five little rocky peaks, none of them presenting any difficulty but sufficiently craggy to be interesting. The highest, Caesteal, is only 2,504 feet in height, but the isolated position of the mountain gives it a dignity and grandeur quite out of proportion to its mere size, and makes it one of the most striking and impressive in all Scotland. Its position also creates a tendency for it to collect clouds, which greatly increase its apparent height, when not so thick as to obscure the outline altogether, but their presence unfortunately prevented the present writer from enjoying the view from the summit, and indeed it was only a sudden small break in the mist that enabled him to see which was the real top. A direct descent by a steep gully where the afore-mentioned ridge opens on to Sgor Chionasaid enables the climber to reach a farm called Ribigill, whence a track leads through the bog to the Tongue road.

The hotel at Tongue, overlooking the Kyle of that name, is the best centre from which to explore this north coast country. The road from Loch Loyal reaches it after passing under some shapely outlying supporters of Ben Loyal. Here the road divides, one part going to the east and the other circling round the Kyle to the west. The eastern road follows the coast for three or four miles to Tongue Bay at the entrance to the Kyle, where there are sandy beaches and dunes (196), and a glimpse of the open sea between the outlying islands. Rising steeply above the road is a little hill called Cnoc-an-Freiceadain, barely 1,000 feet high, which presents a very striking face to the sea with cliffs which, in certain lights, almost recall the Dolomites (195). From this point the road takes a turn inland but runs out again at intervals to the coast, passing Bettyhill, where there is a hotel, and eventually reaches Thurso and John o' Groats.

The north coast between Tongue and Cape Wrath is cut into deeply by the three inlets of the Kyle of Tongue, Loch Eriboll, and the Kyle of Durness, and the roads therefore follow a very serpentine course, but this adds greatly to the interest for those who are not in too great a hurry. On leaving Tongue, the Kyle has first to be circumnavigated, and before rounding the head of the loch a little lakelet, the Lochan Hakel (or Hacoin) is passed, whence the most impressive views of Ben Loyal are obtained. Every time the car paused there seemed to be a fresh effect of cloud and mountain, causing many delays in the interest of photography (208). The remarkable outline of the mountain is well seen from this point and it towers up majestically over the water and surrounding bogs.

After descending to the head of the Kyle the road turns sharply northward and keeps near the shore till it comes opposite the hotel at Tongue, with fine views back to Ben Loyal all the way. At this point a branch goes off to Melness and the coast, while the main road turns west to cross the peninsula between the Kyle of Tongue and Loch Eriboll. Just where it turns there is a particularly fine glimpse of Ben Loyal whose striking outline is seen at its best from this point (209).

Beyond Melness there are fine views across Tongue Bay towards Cnoc-an-Freiceadain (214) and there are big cliffs 800 or 900 feet high in places below the high ground culminating in Ben Hutig (1,340 feet), but they can only be seen by tramping over rather rough country as the road comes to an end at Strath Melness.

After crossing a stretch of moorland the main road descends to Hope Lodge at the foot of Loch Hope, over which rises Ben Hope (3,040 feet), and a branch road turns southward along the loch (215). Next a low ridge is climbed and a sharp descent leads down to Loch Eriboll, another long arm of the sea, and there is a good view of it from the top of the hill overlooking a little rocky island connected with the mainland by a remarkable shingle ridge (210). There used to be a ferry here, but it is not much used now as a modern car covers the ten miles round the head of the loch in little more time than would be lost by the delays attending a ferry crossing. For the tourist the longer route is, of course, preferable as the views across the loch with Ben Hope towering over the intermediate ridges are very pleasant, and there is an interesting Pictish house of unknown antiquity to be visited on the way. It consists of a small underground chamber, approached by a narrow passage, and suggests a very primitive way of life.

To the west of the entrance to Loch Eriboll there is a fascinating piece of coast with fine cliffs of no great height but split up by lovely little coves and sandy bays. Here, those who cannot walk far can at any rate descend from the car and stroll about on the rocks or the beaches. I have seen the sea here as blue as the Mediterranean and flecked with lines of white as the sunlit breakers rolled into the bay. Excellent views can be obtained from a place called Rispond both across the loch to the fine headland known as

Whiten Head (212) and along the broken cliffs and sandy inlets to the west (211). Here there is a typical Highland shop, miles away from the nearest habitation, for in this sparsely populated district people do not go to the shop but the shop to the people. A van is fitted with a back-board which can be lowered to form a kind of counter and the simple requirements of the district stored in the body are taken round from farm to farm or fisherman's cottage as opportunity occurs. The shop itself is thus a kind of storehouse situated on the road at a spot where boats can land heavier cargo.

Further on there is a strange crack in the cliffs forming a narrow inlet with almost perpendicular sides and ending in Smoo Cave, and beyond this again is the little scattered village of Durness, where there is a small inn. Progress to the west is here interrupted by the Kyle of Durness (216), and the road to Cape Wrath can only be reached by a ferry which starts from a place called Keoldale, just off the road to the south. This ferry is a doubtful proposition except at the height of the season, when a public vehicle plies to Cape Wrath, and I doubt whether it is capable of taking a car. Cape Wrath is a fine sheer cliff, but as the road runs inland over featureless moorland a tramp of over twelve miles in each direction is an adventure which only the young and fit are likely to undertake.

The return journey by the western route to Lairg is a run of about fifty-six miles through wild and undeveloped country of much interest. After leaving the Kyle of Durness a stop should be made at Loch Tarbhaidh to admire the view of Foinaven (2,980 feet), which stands up well to the south (213). The road touches the sea at Loch Inchard where there used to be an inn at Rhiconich, and then passes through a strange country of low rocky hills interspersed with innumerable little lochans, which looks as though it ought to be a paradise for the fisherman. Another short run brings us to Laxford Bridge, where the sea is again met at the head of Loch Laxford, and here the ways divide, a branch going off to Scourie, where there is a hotel, and then turning south to the ferry at Kylesku. Scourie should be a good centre from which to explore the coast and the cliffs of Handa Island, the breeding-place of innumerable sea birds, and the coast road provides an alternative route to the south for those who do not mind rough going and the risks of the ferry together with an extra fifteen or twenty miles of travel. The direct route from Laxford Bridge to Lairg is not to be despised as it skirts a chain of lochs backed by ranges of wild mountains which possess individuality and character of their own. The first of any size is Loch Stack, and here again the car should be stopped to enjoy views in more than one direction. Right opposite, across the water, is Arkle (2,580 feet), a bare hill covered with steep screes (217), and to the south-east are a number of heights forming part of Reay Forest which stretches half-way to Lairg. The road skirts the base of Ben Stac (2,364 feet), which is best seen from the next stage at Loch More (218). This is an attractive little pyramid whose fine outline gives it a claim to a higher rank among Scottish hills than its mere height would justify. All these hills would probably repay exploration but their remote position in deer forests at a great distance from any inn or stopping-place, makes them rather inaccessible, and I cannot give any first-hand information about them, but must refer readers to the Scottish Mountaineering Club's Guide-Book to the Northern Highlands. Their marked individuality and their proximity to numerous sheets of water with a background of the sea on the west should make them excellent viewpoints. There appears to be much scree and rough going. Foinaven has some fine crags on the east side, and there is a stalkers' path which greatly helps in the ascent of Ben Stac.

Two more lochs are then followed, Loch Merkland under Ben Hee, and Loch a'Ghriama, before the long and comparatively uninteresting Loch Shin is reached. It is about seventeen miles long, and the shores are nowhere steep, though some occasional interest may be gained by glimpses of Ben More Assynt (3,273 feet) peering over the lower ranges of hills across the loch. Lairg, with its hotel and railway station, is situated at the southern end, and here we reach the point from which we started at the beginning of this chapter. A powerful modern car could perform the whole round of one hundred and twenty miles in a single day with ease, but I hope none of my readers will attempt to do so, as those who travel at such a pace would miss most of the pleasure to be derived from the exploration of this grand country. There are so many places which cry out for delay and detailed exploration, so many spots where even those who lack the walking powers of the members of the Scottish Mountaineering Club can linger with infinite delight, but which can only be reached without prodigious effort by car. This region, therefore, as suggested earlier, is particularly suited for a motor trip, so long as the car is used merely as a means of access and a movable base from which to explore the beauties of the country.

IX

The Isle of Skye

SKYE IS NOWADAYS THE MECCA of the climbing fraternity, and, though for years I had wondered what it was like, I had a notion that it was hardly the place for an ordinary humdrum pedestrian like myself, and that if I went there I should not be able to penetrate into the recesses of the mountains, but should have to contemplate them from afar, and with as much respect as one would the mighty Alpine or Himalayan peaks. Most of the photographs, too, that I had seen gave such a notion of bare rock and utter desolation that they seemed almost repellent. It was indeed only when I had actually visited the Cuillin that I found these ideas to be far from the truth.

It is a fact that these hills differ from almost all others in Britain—except perhaps one or two in Ross—in that there is rarely an easy way to the top. In most places there is usually a back way up to be found, but here the peaks often have no back, and, in consequence, many of them can only be reached by trained climbers armed with ropes and other adjuncts of the craft.

There are, however, various routes across the chain, and a number of summits which are no more than a rough scramble. These are quite sufficient to enable an ordinary hill rambler to obtain a very fair notion of what these mountains are like. The bare rock, too, is there, and here and there—in places like Coire na Creiche—the masses of loose stones and unrelieved ferocity of the rocks are apt to be depressing, but usually the majesty of the rock towers gives a certain grandeur to the landscape, and the bald effect is relieved by patches of heather.

Above all, the proximity to the ocean is an everlasting joy, and the great stretches of sea visible from almost every point of vantage add the colour needed to set off the blackness of the gabbro of which the Cuillin Hills are built. A little snow, too, helps to clothe the nakedness of these crags, and I have been fortunate in making my visits in the early spring, when there was a plentiful supply of this most useful aid to mountain photography.

Skye can be reached by the ferry from Kyle, and though Kyle Akin on the other side is a pretty spot, and the hills above the village are well worth a visit, this is too far from the centre of things for a long stay. The steamer calls at Broadford, which is convenient for the Red Hills, and there is a road to Loch Slapin at the foot of Blaven, but the more usual route to Sligachan is from Portree, whence a good road leads to that famous resort.

Those who have time should spend a few days at Portree, for there are many other things in Skye deserving of a visit besides the Cuillin, and Portree is probably the best centre to work from.

At Easter-time in 1921 we approached Skye under wild wintry conditions. A gale from the north, which alone can stir up these protected waters, lashed the usually calm sound into a miniature English Channel, prevented our calling at Broadford, and made the little *Shiela*, with her seasick passengers and her limited accommodation, anything but a comfortable means of transport. To add to our discomfort a cargo of 500 sheep had been taken aboard and occupied all the spare space on the ship, including the first-class cabin; to which troubles were added sharp snowstorms at intervals, one of them so dense that the boat missed the entrance to Portree harbour altogether, and when the squall had passed had to turn round and retrace its course.

There was a heavy fall of snow in the night and next morning everything was white down to the water's edge, making our proposed expedition up the Storr quite out of the question.

We were able, however, to walk along the cliffs overlooking the entrance to the harbour, and these looked very fine in their white garb (219). Though the outlines of the more distant hills were obscured by cloud, the view across the Sound of Raasay, backed by great snowclouds, was most beautiful. The striking headland in our picture, beyond the harbour entrance on the right, is Ben Tianavaig (1,362 feet), and deserves an expedition to itself as it possesses some extraordinary rock scenery, and, on a clear day, should command a particularly beautiful view. The cliff walk may be continued indefinitely, and there are fine views of the mainland all the way.

Recently a new road has been made between the mountains and the coast which enables the sights of the northern part of the island to be visited by motor-car.

The northern part of the island has a curious backbone of mountain starting north of Portree and running more or less parallel to the coast almost to the end. In places it exceeds 2,000 feet in height, and slopes gradually up from the west, but breaks away in a tremendous escarpment on the east. Except for a few slight depressions there is an almost continuous line of crags for fifteen miles, and in one or two places there are really imposing precipices.

The highest point of the range is the Storr (2,360 feet), and here, in addition to the tremendous main cliffs, there are some extraordinary rock formations (220). The best known of these is the strange obelisk known as the Old Man of Storr (221), which is a landmark from the sea for many miles around. It stands on a pyramidal base of debris, amid a weird collection of rock pinnacles, and is said to be about 160 feet high.

Farther north, almost at the end of the range, is an even more extra-ordinary collection of rocks known as the Quiraing (222). Here a group of huge towers enclose a narrow space at the foot of the cliff, with a flat-topped mass in the middle known as the Table. It is approached by a narrow and steep path from below, and forms a sort of natural castle. Indeed it seems to have been used as a safe retreat in the bad old days. It is difficult to get a satisfactory photograph of it as the rocks are too close together, but our

223 Loch Coruisk from Bealach-na-Glaic-Moire

224 Loch Scavaig

225 Loch Bracadale and Macleod's Tables

226 Coast near the Spar Cave (Strathaird)

227 Dunvegan Head

228 Macleod's Maidens

230 Talisker Cliff

231 Waterstein Head

232   View from Red Hills

233　View from Sgùrr nan Gillean

234 Sgùrr nan Gillean

235 The Cuillin from Bruach na Frithe

236 Loch Scavaig

237 Loch Scavaig

238 Loch Coruisk

239 Loch Coruisk

240 Coruisk and the Cuillin from Sgùrr-na-Stri

241 Sgùrr Alasdair from Loch Brittle

242 Sgùrr na Banachdich from Loch Brittle

243 Loch Brittle

244 Cuillin from Beinn Staic

245 Skye Ponies, Glen Brittle

246 Rudh' an Dunain

247 Rudh' an Dunain and Canna

248 Sgùrr Alasdair from Coire Lagan

249 Sgùrr a' Ghreadaidh

illustration (222), taken from the edge of the slope leading to the top of the mountain, shows the outer pylons guarding the entrance to this strange sanctuary. This photograph was taken on a hot summer day, in extraordinary contrast to the wintry conditions under which we had landed three weeks earlier. A sea mist hung low over the water, through which the islands poked their heads in a strange manner. From all this range of hills there are magnificent views of the distant mainland peaks across the sound.

There is much fine cliff scenery on the western coasts of Skye, which can be seen by the help of a motor from Portree or Dunvegan. There is also a little inn at Carbost and a private hotel open in summer at Orbost on Loch Bracadale. The latter enjoys good distant views of the Cuillin across the water, and Loch Bracadale has an interesting coastline with boldly projecting headlands, little inlets, caves, and several islands. It is well protected and would be an excellent place for those fond of boating to explore (225). There is a splendid walk to Idrigill Point and the three rocky obelisks called Macleod's Maidens (228) standing out in the sea, and this could be prolonged to the northward along the wild and, in places, rather grim cliffs. Two hills of moderate height, called Macleod's Tables, can also be reached, but the walk is apt to be boggy and may not repay the effort, though these hills are conspicuous objects all along this coast as they stand up alone over the rough moorland. Other expeditions from Orbost are best made by car as the front gate is two miles from the house, but all the Dunvegan neighbourhood is within easy reach, and drives can also be made to all the northern parts of the island.

In three places the Skye cliffs rise to a height of about 1,000 feet over the sea, and in one, Dunvegan Head, to 1,026 feet (227). This and Waterstein Head (966 feet) can be approached by rough roads starting from Dunvegan, but the last bit will have to be done on foot. Waterstein (231) can be well seen from neighbouring cliffs with a glimpse of the Outer Hebrides behind it across the Minch. It can also be viewed from a long low peninsula, with a lighthouse on it, partly composed of irregular but broken basaltic columns, which juts out across the bay at its foot.

Tourists who possess a car will, no doubt, wish to visit Dunvegan Castle, which has been the headquarters of the Macleods since the ninth century, with its famous relics and fairy flag, and to drive along the road to the extreme north of the island to the ruins of Duntulm Castle with views of the outer islands across the Minch most of the way. A return may be made by the Quiraing, the basaltic cliffs of Staffin, and under the Old Man of Storr to Portree.

The third high cliff is that at Talisker (937 feet), best visited from the little inn at Carbost on Loch Harport, whence there is a fine glimpse backwards to the Red Hills (229). The great cliffs rise over a pleasant little bay and can best be seen at low tide from the rocks at their base (230), but the cliffs on the other side of the bay are also well worth exploration. Beyond Carbost and its famous distillery there is a settlement of crofters, said to have been brought from the outer isles, who appear to be more enterprising

x*

and prosperous than most of the native inhabitants of Skye. They add to their resources by a number of hand looms where fine home-spun tweeds of the same type as the well-known Harris brand are produced, to a great extent woven from the wool of their own sheep. Visitors to this wild western coast are usually tempted to return with a roll of this famous Port-na-long cloth.

Most visitors will sooner or later make their way to the famous hotel at Sligachan, beloved of climbers, which is the only hostelry from which the Cuillin can be visited. This hotel stands at the entrance to Glen Sligachan, a long and dreary valley full of bog, and shut in between the Red Hills on one side and the Black Cuillin on the other. About half-way along this valley there is a fine glimpse into Harta Corrie, and the latter part, along a little loch and under the towering crags of Blaven, is fine, but the rough and boggy track for the first three or four miles is a weariness to the flesh, especially as it has often to be traversed both on the outward and the return journey.

A very pleasant and easy expedition from Sligachan is to follow the inviting-looking ridge leading up to the Red Hills forming part of Lord Macdonald's Forest. Glamaig (2,537 feet), the highest of these hills, is too steep to be attractive, but the next hill to it is easily attained, and commands splendid views both of the Cuillin opposite and of the sea channels and mainland on the other side. We spent a most enjoyable Sunday here, in fine weather, with glorious clouds and a blue distance—a succession of lazy hours basking in the sunshine and drinking in the beauty of the landscape seen through that magic atmosphere (232).

The Red Hills are formed of a crumbly kind of pink granite. The lower slopes are usually covered with heather, but the tops are bare and bald, and as the watercourses are also stony and bare the hills sometimes look as though someone had emptied a vast pot of red paint over them, which had run down the sides in streaks.

These Red Hills are usually separate from one another, have very steep sides, and tend to copy one another in shape, having a large rounded head and a sharper little tail running out behind. The outlines from the distance are bold and striking, but there are practically no crags, and the only difficulty of ascending any of them lies in the steepness of the loose scree.

Very different are the jagged ridges of the Black Cuillin, standing on the other side of Glen Sligachan. These are the mountains people come to Skye to see, and there is nothing else in our islands to compare with them. They are formed of hard black volcanic gabbro—an ideal rock for climbing, as it is firm and rough, affording a foothold in places which would be absolutely impossible on a softer or more friable rock.

In places there are large slabs of smooth, slippery surface which have caused more than one fatal accident to wanderers who have lost their way, and not infrequently great curved blocks occur like the back of a huge sea monster. The bigger summits are all very much of the same size, but great variety is given by the extraordinary outlines and strange skyline.

Page 82

The best known, and in some ways the finest, peak is Sgùrr nan Gillean (3,167 feet). It stands just at the corner of the range over Sligachan, and in shape is almost the ideal of what a mountain should be. It has a sharp peak supported by a number of jagged pinnacles, and is inaccessible to all but practised climbers on every side save one. From the farther end of Glen Sligachan it presents an outline that reminds one of Lichfield Cathedral with its lofty central and twin western spires.

The only route to the top for non-climbers is found by crossing the bog behind the hotel and making for the ridge to the south of the summit. Once this is reached the hard work is done, and it is a pleasant scramble to the top. In clear weather there is no difficulty, but in bad weather, with a strong wind, or ice on the rocks, care is necessary in one or two narrow places where a slip might have serious consequences. It is perhaps wiser for those who are unused to mountains to be accompanied by an experienced guide, or at any rate by someone who has been up before, now that John McKenzie, almost the only real guide that Scotland has so far produced, is no longer there to help the stranger. It would be easy to get into difficulties were the narrow way missed.

On the day of my visit I was favoured with wonderful weather. The sky was unclouded, and the atmosphere so clear that we could see the Outer Hebrides in one direction and Ben Nevis in the other, while islands like Rum and Eigg, twenty miles away, were seen with clear reflections in the calm, glassy waters of the Atlantic. It was so still that a match burned steadily without shelter, and we sat for an hour or more on the narrow summit, where there is just room for five or six people to repose in comfort, gazing at the scene around us, under conditions rarely met with in the fickle climate of the west.

Though the view is more extensive from the top it is more satisfactory, from the photographic standpoint, from the ridge at the base of the final cone. There is more room there to move about, and to select the foregrounds necessary to the making of a good picture. Our illustration (233) was taken from this lower elevation, and gives the view looking across the lower end of Glen Sligachan towards the western face of Blaven (3,042 feet), the great outlying peak of the black gabbro which stands in isolated grandeur facing the Red Hills. The sharp peak in the middle is Garbh-bheinn (2,649 feet), and between the two is the rugged outline of Clach Glas, the traverse of which is considered a tit-bit for first-class cragsmen. In the middle distance one of the red hills has strayed among the blacks, and in the background are the hills on the mainland, and a glimpse of the entrance to Loch Hourn, commanded by the sentinel peak of Ben Sgriol just to the right of Garbh-bheinn.

By far the best view of Sgùrr nan Gillean is obtained from the ridge leading to Sgùrr a' Bhasteir, the lower peak jutting out to the right of the big mountain, as seen from Sligachan. It is easily reached from the corries on either side, and may be combined with the ascent of Bruach na Frithe (3,143 feet) by working round the extraordinary rock towers known as Am Basteir, or the

Executioner, and the Bhasteir Tooth (which should surely be called the Axe).

From this point the sharp summit of Sgùrr nan Gillean towers up magnificently above the supporting pinnacles, and when the gullies are filled with snow, as is often the case on these northern slopes quite late into the season, it is difficult to believe that this is a Scottish hill-top and not some mighty Alpine peak (234).

It is fortunate for the non-climber that the finest view in the whole range is that from Bruach na Frithe, which is the most accessible of all the bigger peaks. It is easily reached from Sligachan, either by following the ridge all the way up from the pass leading to Glen Brittle, or better still, by going straight up from the corrie between it and Sgùrr a' Bhasteir (Fionn Choire). There are no difficulties beyond the steepness and the vast quantities of loose stones which cannot be avoided anywhere in the Cuillin.

What gives this view its special effectiveness is the way the main ridge twists round, giving the appearance of three ridges, one in front of the other. Each is crowned with a series of rock towers of which the most important is Bidein Druim nan Ramh (2,900 feet), the Matterhorn of the district.

When our photograph (235) was taken there was a slight haze which helped to pick out the separate ridges, and made the big mountains in the distance look farther off, and consequently higher. The three main peaks in our picture are Sgùrr Dearg (3,254 feet) on the right, Sgùrr Alasdair (3,309 feet) in the middle, and Sgùrr Dubh (3,089 feet) on our left. I give the Ordnance Survey heights, though an article in *The Scottish Mountaineering Club Journal* for 1923 shows good reason for doubting the accuracy of some of them.[1]

Some years ago the above-mentioned club published a large-scale map of these hills, a copy of which is hanging up in the hotel at Sligachan. In it are marked the various routes and passes; these are drawn in different colours, and graded according to their difficulty or importance. Those who intend to explore the innermost recesses of the hills should study this map carefully before starting, and, in doubtful weather, should take pains to note the way they have come, as weather-changes in these parts are very sudden, particularly as there may be only one way down that will not land the inexperienced wanderer in difficulties.

After studying the map we found a route, marked as reasonable, over the pass between Bidein and Sgùrr a' Mhadaidh, called the Bealach na Glaic Moire, which would enable us to obtain some notion of the hills beyond the middle ridge seen from Bruach na Frithe.

It is some distance from Sligachan to the bottom of the pass in Coire na Creiche, at the head of which is a great rocky buttress dividing the corrie into two parts. The right-hand one of these, called Tairneilear, has to be climbed, and from this a steep gully, full of huge rocks and snow, leads to the top of the pass. The scramble up the long gully is very tiring, but when this has been negotiated a short detour to the right leads to the ridge, which can be traversed for some little distance in either direction.

[1] The corrected heights given in the Guide are Sgùrr Dearg 3,206 feet, Sgùrr Alasdair 3,251 feet, and Bidein Druim nan Ramh 2,850 feet.

The view from this ridge is very striking (223), for one can look down into the desolate, rock-girt hollow in which lies the famous Loch Coruisk. The hill commanding the farther end of the lake is Sgùrr-na-Stri (1,623 feet), a splendid viewpoint, and beyond is the sea, with one long promontory after another jutting out into it.

It is also possible to ascend Sgùrr na Banachdich (3,167 feet) from Sligachan, but it is such a long walk round the base of all the buttresses of this irregular chain of mountains that it is better tackled from Glen Brittle, if accommodation can be got there. *hotel at least now*

The great expedition from Sligachan is to traverse the whole length of the Glen to Camasunary (Camas Fhionnairidh), a delightful little bay between Sgùrr-na-Stri and Blaven (which, by the way, would make an ideal site for an hotel), and then to follow the coast round Sgùrr-na-Stri, with its glorious views over Loch Scavaig, past the notorious 'Bad Step', which can easily be avoided by clambering a little up the hillside, and so on to Loch Coruisk, and back over the Druim Hain ridge to Glen Sligachan.

This means a long round of over twenty miles, and visitors sometimes content themselves with the walk to Coruisk and back by the same path over the ridge, but by so doing they miss the most beautiful part of all.

The day we had for our walk by Loch Scavaig was most satisfactory. There was bright sunshine over the sea, whilst some heavy clouds hung over the western chain of hills, and over Coruisk, giving that sense of gloom which is so appropriate to that wild loch.

Scavaig was looking extraordinarily beautiful in the sunshine. The clear sea-water danced and sparkled among the rocks, while Gars Bheinn (2,934 feet), the end peak of the Cuillin range, loomed dark and stern across the loch, with an angry cloud rolling over its summit.

About half-way along the shelf on which the path runs there projects a little headland which commands what I feel I may claim to be the grandest view in Britain (236). All around steep bare precipices descend into the sea, and through a gap in them a glimpse is seen of the fresh-water Loch Coruisk with its girdle of black cliffs, backed by the jagged peaks of the Cuillin. The highest points are obscured by clouds in our picture, but the Bidein in the centre is almost clear, and the sharp peak of Sgùrr nan Gillean and the weird outline of the Executioner are peeping over the middle ridge.

The sombre effect of all this bare rock is tempered by the wonderful colour of the sea, clear as crystal on this rocky shore, and toned to a pale green under the lee of the little island in the centre. There is, too, a certain amount of vegetation even here; every crack and cranny is filled with heather, and down on our shelf by the water, where the diminished steepness allows a little earth to accumulate, there is a veritable rock garden (237). These photographs were taken in May, and here, among the stones, was a profusion of ferns and wild flowers, primroses, bluebells, violets, and orchids, which made the wilderness blossom as the rose, and served as an admirable foil to the savage mountains beyond.

Crossing the narrow spit of land that separates the two lochs the walker finds himself in even sterner and more savage surroundings. Though Scott's poetic description may be somewhat exaggerated, and patches of heather, and even an occasional wild flower, may be found in the crannies of the rocks, Coruisk is certainly the wildest of our British lakes, and the prevailing impression it leaves behind is one of naked crags, black water, and piles of stones (238).

Coruisk should be seen on a dull day, with heavy clouds about, if it is to appear in its most impressive mood, but the clouds should not be too low as the mountain outline is worth having in the picture. The head of the loch is dominated by Sgùrr a' Ghreadaidh, supported on either side by Sgùrr a' Mhadaidh and Sgùrr na Banachdich. Nearer at hand Sgùrr Dubh towers up above the inky water (239), its shape curiously repeated by a series of lesser heights in front.

Sgùrr-na-Stri (1,623 feet) may be climbed without difficulty by following the ridge from the place where the Sligachan-Coruisk path crosses it. The detour is well worth making as this little mountain has a fine rocky summit, with steep crags sloping down into the sea. It is so situated as to command an almost complete view of the range with all its famous peaks grouped round the deep-set hollow in which Coruisk reposes (240). This belvedere can also be ascended direct from Camasunary by an obvious gully leading up to the ridge where it joins the other route to the top, but the stream at the bottom may have to be waded, as there is no bridge, and in springtime the water can be cold!

The best centre from which to explore the farther side of the Cuillin is Glen Brittle, and, as it was not the regular holiday season, we were fortunate in finding comfortable quarters in a cottage by the sea. This limited accommodation is much sought after, and therefore needs no advertisement, so that I refrain from publishing the name of our capable and obliging hostess.

As we purposed a stay of a fortnight or more we had to study the problem of transport, luggage being difficult to convey to this remote spot. Mine host at the Portree hotel hesitated to risk his own car on the mountain road from Carbost, but succeeded in finding an old Ford which accomplished the journey for us without serious mishap. From the end of the road we had to carry our bags slung on walking-sticks for another half-mile to our cottage, mostly through bog, as the bridge had recently been washed away and re-erected farther up, without any regular approach to it from either side.

It was a most uncomfortable drive in bitter wind and driving snow, but we were fortunate in arriving when we did as we had an opportunity of seeing the Cuillin under deep snow—a great chance for the photographic enthusiast.

Next morning the sun came out and an entrancing vision presented itself to our gaze. Right opposite our windows, across the loch, Sgùrr Alasdair, the highest peak of the range, raised its sharp peak to the white clouds which were sweeping across the blue sky and here and there touching the mountain-tops (241). To the left was Sgùrr Dearg, then Banachdich, and the rest, all gleaming in a mantle of fresh snow (242).

These conditions meant postponing more serious expeditions among the mountains for a day or two, but they were well worth it, for the view of the mountains from the coast under their white mantle was superb.

Plate 243 shows Loch Brittle under more normal conditions, when much of the snow had melted; a brisk sea breeze was driving long lines of foaming breakers into the little bay, and threatening banks of cloud were forming along the mountain-tops.

It has always been my ambition to find a holiday resort where sea and mountain are combined, and Glen Brittle fulfils this ideal as well as any other place I know. It possesses more open sea than most of the Highland lochs, and, besides the expeditions among the Cuillin Hills, there are very beautiful cliff walks when the weather is too unsettled for mountaineering. A few miles to the west there are high cliffs 600 to 700 feet high, with fine views across the water to Rum, and along the coast towards Talisker, where the cliffs are nearly 1,000 feet high.

The hills on the west side of the glen are also worth a visit. One afternoon, when it had cleared up after a wet morning, but too late for a long walk, we made our way up Beinn Staic (1,347 feet), from which there is an excellent panorama of the outer side of the main range of the Cuillin (244). In the illustration, and beginning on the left, we see Mhadaidh, Ghreadaidh, Banachdich and Dearg, the latter with a snowy summit which hides the famous Inaccessible Pinnacle, the actual top of the mountain. This picture shows clearly the way up Banachdich, which provides one of the easiest ascents for the non-climber. This route more or less follows the long snow-filled crack leading right up to the shoulder of the mountain.

There are also delightful walks along the opposite, or south-eastern, shore of Loch Brittle, all of which are suitable for unsettled or doubtful weather. The stretch of bog between the sea and the hills is dull, but may be enlivened by a troop of shaggy Skye ponies turned loose to find what sustenance they can in this inhospitable country (245). The walk along the shore, however, is interesting all the way; little rocky coves and headlands remind one of Cornwall, and the cliff scenery, towards the end of the point called Rudh' an Dunain, or Castle Point, is of a high order (246). Remains of an ancient fortification wall, six or eight feet thick, stretching across the end of the promontory, have given it its name. When this was built the headland probably extended farther, as the space now enclosed seems hardly large enough to warrant such an elaborate protection.

These cliffs are not very high, but I am inclined to think that sea cliffs are more enjoyable when one is not too far above the water. It is pleasant to be near enough to see the clear blue water surging among the rocks, or, in stormy weather, to watch the waves dashing themselves into spray against this iron-bound coast.

The mountains of Rum, too, are a great object of interest all along these cliffs, and looked particularly fascinating after the heavy snowfall on our first arrival. Canna is less interesting, but even this comparatively flat island looks attractive in certain lights (247).

By cutting across the bog and following the coast it is possible to walk right round Gars Bheinn to Scavaig and Coruisk. The walk is a fine one, and enables the rarely visited western side of those lochs to be seen.

Some of the corries on the Loch Brittle side of the Cuillin are as fine as any. Before the snow melted we made our way up to Coire Lagan, under the crags of Sgùrr Alasdair and Sgùrr Mhic Choinnich. In these wintry conditions the scene looked quite Alpine (248), and the mountains appeared very formidable. The stone shoot, which is said to provide the only easy way up Alasdair, looked so steep and forbidding in the snow that we decided to leave it alone, a holiday being meant for pleasure rather than for hard and exacting toil.

We studied the easy route up Banachdich when looking at it from Beinn Staic, as mentioned a few pages back. There are one or two steep pitches, and an interminable number of stones large and small, but no other difficulties. The summit is a narrow ridge with tremendous precipices on the inner side, and pretty steep slopes on the outer. There are also good views of the neighbouring heights.

On our way down, and just before leaving the ridge, some thin clouds floated up from the sea and wreathed themselves round the mountains, producing some very striking effects, and adding enormously to the apparent scale of the peaks. Sgùrr a' Ghreadaidh, for instance, seemed at times almost to take upon itself the form of Monte Rosa as seen from the Monte Moro Pass, and it was difficult to persuade oneself that this was really in Scotland, and a mountain not much over 3,000 feet high (249).

The mountains towards the south end of the chain are usually more easily climbed than those farther north, though this advantage is partly offset by their greater distance from any possible base of operations.

Sgùrr Dearg can be reached from the Bealach Coire na Banachdich, or by the long ridge running up straight from Glen Brittle; though I must confess to a failure on the latter route, as we hesitated to attack the narrower part of the upper ridge in the tremendous gale then blowing, especially as we were hampered by the considerable amount of snow which still covered the rocks.

The Inaccessible Pinnacle, of course, must be left to expert climbers. This extraordinary horn rises from a ridge some way below what ought to be the top of the mountain, but it is a few feet higher, being the second summit of the whole chain.

Sgùrr Sgumain, whose crags on the Glen Brittle side afford plenty of opportunities for the rock-climbing enthusiast, can be scaled from the end of the ridge or from Coir' a Ghrunnda, but perhaps the most repaying is Sgùrr-nan-Eag (3,037 feet), the ascent of which, from the back, requires nothing more than the usual expenditure of breath and energy needed for any of the steep and stony slopes of the Cuillin (250).

The view from this summit of Sgùrr Alasdair, towering up over Coir' a Ghrunnda, with its little lake at the bottom set in its stony basin, is very striking (251). This wild corrie should be visited for its own sake. It is quite a scramble to get into it from below, but there is no risk if the right way is

250 Blaven and Coruisk from Sgùrr-nan-Eag

251 Sgùrr Alasdair and Coir' a Ghrunnda from Sgùrr-nan-Eag

252 Cuillin from Elgol

253　Loch Scavaig and the Cuillin from Elgol

254 Blaven from Loch Slapin

255 Ben Sgriol and Mainland from Loch-na-Dal

256 Rum from Point of Sleat

257 Blaven from Ord

Y

258 Cuillin from Ord—Sunset

260. Red and Black Cuillin from Gauscavaig

261 Loch-na-Keal and Beinn Talaidh

262 Loch-na-Keal and Ben More

263 Loch-na-Keal and Ben More

264 Loch-na-Keal and Beinn Fhada

265 Loch-na-Keal and Ben More

266 Loch-na-Keal

267 Loch-na-Keal—Entrance

268 Ben More—Summit

269 Loch Spelve

270　Ben More from Loch Scridain

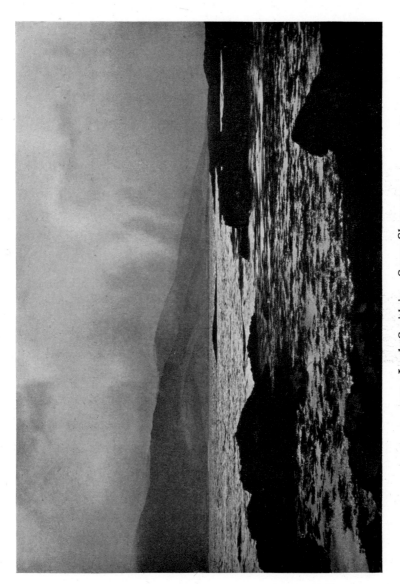

271 Loch Scridain—Snow Showers

272   Ben More from Frozen Lochan

273 Loch Bà
274 Frozen waterfall on Ben More

taken. This lies well up the hillside on the left, but even experienced climbers have got themselves into difficulties in bad weather by trying to follow the natural course by the stream at the bottom, where the way is blocked by smooth, slippery slabs by no means easy to negotiate.

From Sgùrr-nan-Eag the ridge walk to Gars Bheinn looks very inviting, and the views ought to be very good, but we had used up all our plates on Sgùrr-nan-Eag, and had spent so long over our photography that we had not time to put the matter to the test.

The best general view of the Cuillin is obtained from Elgol, a small village situated on the long promontory that runs south from Blaven, and limited accommodation can be obtained here. The backbone of this peninsula consists of rather featureless moorland, though it commands fine views all round, but the rocky coast, rising in places to real cliffs, provides scenery of a very high order, to which the clear waves of the western sea gurgling among the boulders add a special charm. When in addition to this there is the splendid view across the bay of the grandest mountain outline in Britain, it will easily be realized what a perfect place this is in which to wander about and watch the showers sweeping across the noble hills across the water. In our picture (253) the mountain on the right is Blaven; next it is Marsco rising over Camasunary at the end of Glen Sligachan. The shapely little peak in the middle is Sgùrr-na-Stri, with the main ridge of the Cuillin fading into the cloud on the left. Gars Bheinn stands up as a fine pyramid from this point and makes a worthy end of the long range of the Cuillin over the sea. The rest of the jagged peaks, flecked with snow in the gullies, are those which enclose Loch Coruisk (252) till we come to Sgùrr-na-Stri and continue in (253).

The drive to Elgol from Broadford passes under Beinn-na-Caillich, one of the Red Hills, past a little loch to Torran, and then skirts Loch Slapin, one of the deep indentations made by the sea into this most irregularly-shaped island. From Torran Blaven, supported by the jagged crest of Clach-Glas, beloved of rock-climbers, presents its grandest face—surely one of the finest mountain forms in Britain! (254). It is well worth while to walk for some distance along the east side of Loch Slapin to enjoy this splendid group from slightly different angles and in varied settings. The views back from the west side towards Belig, Garbh-bheinn, and the Red Hills, also disclose a fine and varied mountain outline.

Blaven can be climbed from Loch Slapin by its southern ridge without serious difficulty, and there is a path across the moorland at its base to Camasunary on Loch Scavaig, where the tracks from Sligachan to Loch Coruisk by the 'Bad Step' can be picked up, or the ascent of Sgùrr-na-Stri, described on p. 86, can be undertaken. There is also a pleasant view of Rum over the sea, though the outline is less striking than from farther south.

The southern portion of the Isle of Skye, called Sleat, lies off the usual beat of the tourist, but although it lacks the more dramatic features of the middle of the island it possesses charms of its own of no mean order. These consist, perhaps, more in the views to be had from it than for any special

z

beauties of its own, but it makes a fine platform from which to look across the water both towards the Cuillin and towards the mainland. The coast-line, too, is rocky and of sufficient interest to provide a good foreground for the noble prospect across the sea.

The road to Armadale branches south from that from the ferries at Kyleakin and Kylerhea, a few miles short of Broadford, and as it descends towards the coast at Isleornsay a magnificent view opens up towards the entrance to Loch Hourn, dominated by its sentinel peak of Sgriol (3,196 feet) (255). Where the road turns inland it is always worth while to follow the line of the shore wherever possible as the views across the Sound of Sleat are delightful all the way to Armadale and beyond, as those arriving by the boat from Mallaig on a fine day will be the first to realize. From the cliffs, however, they are always better than from a boat as the extra elevation gives better proportion to the distant hills.

Armadale Castle, the seat of the Macdonalds, stands in wooded and park-like country, in strong contrast to the barren and wild grandeur of most of the island. It is worth while to prolong the expedition to the Point of Sleat at the extreme southern tip of the island, though the last few miles will probably have to be done on foot as the road gradually peters out. The coast at the point is bold and rocky with cliffs with strangely contorted strata though of no great height, and there are grand views across the sea to the finely outlined mountains of Rum (256) as well as northward towards the Cuillin.

A little south of Isleornsay a rough but practicable road runs across to the west coast to a place called Ord, where there is a pleasant little boarding-house. This is an ideal retreat for an artist or for those who are content to contemplate a superb view without requiring violent exercise. There are no mountains to climb, but it is very pleasant to stroll along the cliffs and explore the little bays and headlands with the ever-changing mists and light effects playing about the wild peaks of the Cuillin across the waters of Loch Eishort. Blaven is especially effective, but the long line of the more distant range ending in the sharp peak of Gars Bheinn is also well seen as the inter-vening Strathaird promontory is low and does not hide them (257). The view is not unlike that from Elgol but more distant, while the Blaven group and the Red Hills are nearer and display better their characteristic outlines. The sunsets here are particularly well seen across the water. I remember one specially when the sun had just dipped below the jagged ridge of the Cuillin and lit up the clouds with a fiery red which made the hills look as though ringed with flames. No monochrome photograph can do full justice to such a scene, but (258) may serve as a basis on which the imagination must build up the full glory of such a moment.

A very bad road serves the sparsely populated district to the south, but it leads to two excellent points of view in the bays of Gauscavaig and Tarska-vaig (259). At the former are the crumbling ruins of Dun Scaich, from which the Cuillin view is particularly fine, while from the latter Blaven forms a fine background to the rocky reefs which jut out into the sea and separate the little sandy beaches. Looking back from the road the Red Hills form a noble group with Blaven and its neighbours, Garbh-bheinn and Belig, across the Ob Gauscavaig, and provide as varied a mountain outline as can be found anywhere in Britain (260).

This has, I am afraid, been a very inadequate description of Skye, both with pen and picture, for the island deserves a volume to itself. But, unfortunately, the cost of photographic reproduction sets its limits upon inclination, and I have, in consequence, attempted to give only a bare description of those scenes actually selected for illustration. I must therefore refer any of my readers who want a detailed account to the recently published volume on Skye forming part of *The Scottish Mountaineering Club Guide-Book*. They may also satisfy their curiosity as to the rock-climbing possibilities of the island by consulting Mr. George Abraham's book, or the numerous articles in climbing journals.

I hope, however, that even this modest contribution will help to fill a gap, and, with the help of the photographs, will serve better than anything that has yet appeared to bring before the ordinary nature lover the charm of this wonderful island and the mainland opposite which it lies.

X

Mull and Iona

F ROM KILCHOAN TO THE NEAREST point of Mull is not much more than three miles, though it is five or six to Tobermory, the first point of call of the steamer which plies between Oban and the outer isles on certain days of the week. Tobermory is prettily situated on its little harbour, and has attracted searchers for lost treasure from the great Spanish galleon wrecked there at the time of the Armada, from which some cannon were recovered many years ago. The whole of the northern part of the island is, however, comparatively low, and apart from a rocky coast and the views across the water, which always have a certain charm in this favoured region, it possesses little special attraction for the tourist. The latter will be well advised to continue the pleasant sail down the Sound of Mull for another nine or ten miles to Salen, where there is an excellent small hotel. Most visitors will, of course, arrive from Oban, whence there is a more frequent service, performed at the time of my visit by a weird-looking craft, which was one of the first of such boats to be fitted with a Diesel engine.

At Salen the island is almost cut in two by the deep inlet of Loch-na-Keal, which runs in from the west. The isthmus is not much over three miles across, and marks the boundary between the moorland waste of the northern half of the island from the mountain ranges of the southern. Geologists tell us that this part of Mull was once a mighty volcano at least 10,000 feet high, the shattered ruins of which, worn down by the rains of hundreds of thousands of years, form the complicated hill system we have come to see. The outcrop of basaltic rock which forms some of the most striking cliff scenery, especially on the west coast, is the plainest evidence of this remote volcanic activity. The fluted columnar structure of these basalt rocks is best seen in the cliffs of the little island of Staffa, which lies off the west coast opposite the entrance to Loch-na-Keal (275), and a visit to these and to Fingal's Cave, with its walls of crystallized rock, is one of the regular steamer excursions from Oban in the summer.

Salen is the only practicable base from which to explore the hill district of Mull, the little inn at Pennyghael, on Loch Scridain, being too inaccessible, besides the fact that when we proposed a short visit one April we found that the owners had not sufficient enterprise to open it so far out of the regular season. The Salen hotel, for obvious reasons, is situated close to the steamer pier, overlooking the Sound of Mull. Roads run north along the coast to

Page 92

Tobermory and south to Loch Spelve and Loch Buie, and offer pleasant strolls for doubtful weather beside the sea, though the hills on the opposite side of the sound are not sufficiently lofty or striking in outline to place the scenery in the front rank. About two miles to the east of Salen, at a place called Pennygown, there is a ruined chapel of considerable antiquity, though there are not sufficient architectural features left to enable it to be dated with any accuracy. The most interesting feature in it is the shaft of a cross carved with a ship and a well-executed foliage scroll on one side, and the Madonna and Child on the other. It is apparently of fourteenth-century date, and it is interesting to see how long the old Iona traditions lasted in this remote area, the general form having changed very little in five hundred years, and the late date being indicated only by the details.

For exploring the hills it would have been more convenient if the Salen hotel had been placed on the other side of the isthmus, on the shores of Loch-na-Keal, as the tramp of three or four miles of moderately interesting road at the beginning and end of the majority of the walks is apt to become monotonous. The road divides at the head of the loch, one branch running along the shore on each side of the water. That on the north side is the most delightful stroll in the island. Though there is nothing particularly striking in the immediate foreground the shore is pleasantly varied with rocks and seaweed, and rises to form low cliffs as it approaches the open sea, while islands break up the surface of the loch. But the chief glory of the scene is to be found in the grand and varied outlines of the great hills on the southern side, which rise into fine peaks one behind another, until they culminate in Ben More (3,169 feet), the monarch of the island. Near the head of the loch there is a deep depression between the hills occupied by the fresh-water Loch Bà, which is well worth a visit, and behind which rises the isolated dome of Beinn Talaidh (2,496 feet), a prominent feature in the landscape from all round (261).

It is tempting to multiply illustrations of this most attractive scene, but (261 to 267) must suffice to give some notion of its beauty. On the occasion of our visit to Mull we were plagued by a spell of strong cold easterly gales, which made the hill-tops and ridges too uncomfortable for real enjoyment, and we returned again and again to the lovely shores of Loch-na-Keal, whence, crouching behind a rock for protection from the icy blast, we could watch the splendid pageant of the sky as the clouds rolled above the peaks opposite in an ever-changing picture. Sometimes after a cold shower the sun would break through the black raincloud and light up a long blanket of low-lying mist resting on the summit ridge of Ben More (262); sometimes the peaks stood out clear against a background of towering cumulus (263), and sometimes the heavy clouds sailed across the blue, casting shadows alternating with patches of sunshine to give variety and life to the landscape (264). At other times the cold blast lashed even the narrow waters of the loch, nowhere much over two miles wide, into angry lines of miniature Atlantic breakers, flecking the whole surface with little jets of foam and splashing fiercely over half-submerged rocks (265 and 266).

On another day, when the wind had abated, we explored the low cliffs nearer the entrance to the loch, and looked across the low-lying island of Inch Kenneth to the distant rocks of Staffa, and admired the bold basalt bastions of the cliffs which bound the southern shore (267).

The first hill walk we had was made to the flat-topped peak forming the background to the deep hollow shown in (264). It is the culmination of the long ridge running back from the loch, known as Beinn Fhada (2,304 feet). We chose it as likely to command a fine view over the much-indented coast and as a point of vantage from which to spy out the easiest route by which to attack Ben More. It provided a pleasant ramble, though the east-wind type of weather robbed the atmosphere of that brilliant sparkle and clear distance which are required to show off the west coast at its best. But the most remarkable sight we found was a little lochan not far below the ridge facing Ben More, which afforded astonishing testimony to the rigour of the icy blast which had tormented us down below on the previous day. It was frozen solid, and even the ripples and lines of foam raised by the squall were petrified, as though a sudden spell had been cast upon them. Balls of ice like white marbles also clustered upon the grass and heather of the banks where the water had been blown clean out of the pool (272).

Ben More was a rather longer expedition; the distance as the crow flies from Salen is about seven miles, but the route to either side of the mountain winds about so much that the actual distance to be traversed is probably nearer ten. We decided that the most interesting approach would be by Glen Clachaig, which runs up into the hills from the birch-clad shores of Loch Bà (273), and after traversing the mountain to descend by the long ridge leading down to the shores of Loch-na-Keal, where a car was to meet us and save the six- or seven-mile road tramp at the end of the day. After leaving Loch Bà the way led through a somewhat desolate valley by an intermittent and, in places, boggy track, and then after leaving it at the highest point, over rough and stony ground to the foot of the mountain itself. The last ascent, as is not unusual in the west, looked very formidable as we approached it, but the difficulties smoothed out as we reached them and there was nothing worse to face than a few steep pitches. The summit ridge runs along a fine precipice, edged when we were there with a snow-cornice, which added greatly to its impressiveness, and the view over the long promontories and islands gave a very good idea of the marvellously indented outline of the wild west coast (268).

It is a curious fact that it was comparatively calm on the summit though a cold wind was blowing elsewhere. Possibly the gale striking the precipice was shot upwards, leaving a quieter space along the edge, but as soon as we had made our way to the long ridge by which we had to descend we were met by one of the most piercingly cold blasts it has ever been my misfortune to meet. We turned up our collars and fairly ran along the ridge until a more practicable slope allowed us to throw ourselves over the side in order to get some protection from the icy gale. It was easy to realize how the frozen ripples illustrated in (272) had been formed. On such occasions an old-fashioned deer-stalker's cap with ear-flaps to tie under the chin, or a motor-cyclist's leather helmet, is a great comfort, though on a warm day they are by no means ideal headgear for a mountain walk. Even when we had got half-way down the cold remained intense, and all the little waterfalls were frozen solid and were hung with festoons of long icicles, an unusual condition of April in a hill whose base is swept by the Gulf Stream (274).

From the bottom, where the car was waiting, there is a pleasant view across the loch, especially when the sun is setting over the entrance, but the outlines of the hills, apart from the basalt cliffs on the left, have no special appeal, and the islands which dot the horizon do not rise to any considerable elevation.

The coast road from Salen, after passing Pennygown and the rather dreary Glen Forsa, runs along for ten or twelve miles between the hills and the sound. These hills rise to a height of between 2,000 and 2,500 feet, and look as though they ought to provide a very interesting ridge-walk, though the summits are perhaps too blunt to be called a real ridge, and might prove boggy in places. The views across the sound and towards the more distant mainland in one direction, and over the tangled ridges to Ben More in the other, ought to be fine, but I cannot speak with first-hand knowledge as our easterly gales did not make ridge-walking very attractive, and our exploration of this region was therefore very perfunctory.

On reaching Duart, on the east coast of the island, where there is a ruined castle, an ancient stronghold of the Maclean chiefs, the road turns south, and after passing Loch Spelve makes its way through to Loch Buie, where it stops.

Loch Spelve is a curious hammer-shaped sea-loch running parallel with the coast and connected with the sea by a narrow channel near its middle, which forms the handle of the hammer. From its head Glen Lussa runs up into the hills and provides a pleasant stroll, but the best viewpoint is on the hills over the entrance (269). The hills on the other side are finely grouped, culminating in Creach-bheinn (2,289 feet), which rises over a number of intervening ridges. To the east there is also an extensive view across the broad Firth of Lorne to the mainland towards Oban, backed by the twin peaks of Cruachan. With the new infra-red plates and a telephoto lens it might be possible to make an effective picture of a distant view like this, but with ordinary equipment this could be done only under exceptionally favourable conditions. But the new process is of more scientific than artistic importance: the over-correction of the colours produces an unnatural effect, and even the telephoto lens does not seem to me to be of much value for landscape work under ordinary circumstances, though a lens of about double the usual focus is useful now and then. In the same way a telescope is useful for picking out details, but the view as it appears to the naked eye is really what we wish to record.

The road along the south shore of Loch-na-Keal follows the base of the mountains to the entrance of the loch about ten miles from Salen, bends round under the fluted bastions of the basalt cliffs which we admired from the other side (267), and then cuts through a narrow defile to Loch Scridain, another long sea-loch, which runs in from the west on the south side of Ben More. Thence the road circles the head of the loch to Pennyghael, about twenty miles from Salen, near which is a little inn, which we found closed in April and unable to do more for us than provide tea. The only way, therefore, to explore this side of the island was to hire a car to take us there in the morning and bring us back after tea.

Loch Scridain is well worth a visit, the finest views being obtainable from the south side near the head. Though the mountain outlines fall far short in grandeur of those seen from the sister Loch-na-Keal, Ben More stands up well across the water, with two tent-shaped spurs supporting its right flank. With a sprinkling of fresh snow and fine clouds skimming the summit, as they were doing on that day, Ben More proudly asserted its dignity as undisputed monarch of Mull (270). Farther inland a row of more rounded hills made a softer but entirely satisfactory background to the ruffled waters and rocky shores of the loch. Our expedition was well timed from a photographic point of view, as the weather became very unsettled, with heavy showers of snow and hail, interspersed with bright sunny intervals. This type of weather may bring discomfort at times, and might be disastrous for a high-level expedition, but from a scenic point of view is probably the grandest of all. It is a fascinating game to sally forth from a temporary shelter with a camera when the sun bursts through between the showers and hunt the storm-effects as the heavy clouds roll over the hills, or little swirls of snow or hail catch an errant gleam of sunshine as they sweep across the landscape (271). Under such conditions photography tends to partake of the nature of a sport as well as an art. A quick eye is needed to select a suitable mixture of rock and sea to serve as a setting for the storm beyond, and it is easy to miss the critical moment when the effect is at its best by waiting for a slight improvement, or to be caught changing the plate or film or setting the shutter when a sudden beauty is revealed just after making an exposure. The clouds have a provoking way of promising to clear an opening just where the sun is wanted to break through and then closing up at the critical moment for which one has been waiting for some time. If, too, the sunlight is wanted in two parts of the landscape it has a way of coming first on one and then on the other, so that it is difficult to get the effect one wants, and there are many misses and disappointments. A successful result, however, secured in this type of weather is far more interesting than one taken under ordinary fine-day conditions, and lucky is the man who has plenty of plates with him on the rare days when such chances are to be found! It is because the hail and snow showers interspersed with bright sunshine are most frequently met with a north-west wind in the spring that I so often repeat my claim that the early months of the year are the best for a visit to the Western Highlands.

From Pennyghael a rough cart-track leads across the hills to the southern coast, which is reached in a little over three miles, at a place called Carsaig. Here there is a little triangular cultivated strath, shut in by steep hills ending

275 Basalt Cliffs, Staffa
276 Coast near Carsaig

277 Iona, St. Oran's Chapel

278 Iona—St. Martin's Cross   279 Iona—Doorway in Cathedral

281 Glen Sannox and Cir Mhòr

282 View from Goat Fell

283 View from Goat Fell

284 Cir Mhòr from North Ridge of Goat Fell

285 Beinn Tarsuinn from Peak of the Castles

286 Cir Mhòr from Peak of the Castles

287   Goat Fell from Peak of the Castles

288 Goat Fell from Brodick—Showers

289 Goat Fell from Brodick

290 Holy Island, Lamlash
291 Ridges from Beinn Tarsuinn

292 Beinn Bharrain from North Ridge of Goat Fell
293 View from Suidhe Fhearghas

294 Cioch-na-h'Oighe

295 Cir Mhòr from Glen Rosa

296 Suidhe Fhearghas from Beinn a'Chliabhain

in a bold cliff on the western side some 700 feet high. The coast in both directions is worth exploration, and the tumbled chaos of rocks is sometimes varied by the almost architectural forms of basalt precipices. Three or four miles farther west are the Carsaig Arches, which are said to be fine, but I cannot speak of them with first-hand knowledge as the failure to obtain night quarters at the inn on Loch Scridain left time for only a cursory visit to this coast if we were to get back punctually to the car waiting to take us back to Salen. The weather too had calmed down, and lost the exciting character it had displayed earlier in the day at Loch Scridain, and we had to content ourselves with exploring the iron-bound coast to the east of Carsaig (276).

The southern portion of Mull juts out in a long peninsula to the west, known as the Ross of Mull. It rises to no great height anywhere, but the granite and basalt formations of the sea-cliffs lend a certain interest, while the views across Loch Scridain and the islands possess considerable charm. The modern road skirting the southern shore of Loch Scridain ends at Fionphort, whence the ferry leads to the historic island of Iona, and replaces the ancient pilgrim way, though the modern tourist usually makes his pilgrimage with the help of an excursion steamer from Oban.

This is not the place for a lengthy historical or archaeological account of the sacred isle, but the two or three photographs reproduced here may have some antiquarian value, as they were taken as long ago as 1899, and show the Cathedral Church in its ruined state, before modern restorers put a new roof over it and made it fit again for public worship.

When St. Columba landed here in the year 563 he was not the first Christian missionary to preach in Scotland, for nearly a hundred and seventy years earlier we learn from the Venerable Bede that St. Ninian had built his church at Whithorn (Candida Casa), in Galloway, and converted the southern Picts. St. Patrick's mission to Ireland did not take place till 432, the year of St. Ninian's death. St. Columba's work, however, transcends the other in importance, as his fiery energy established centres of Christian teaching all over northern Scotland, while Aidan of Lindisfarne was sent direct from Iona to establish the Celtic Church in Northumbria at the request of King Oswald, who himself had spent some years of his youth in the sacred isle. We have already (p. 41) described the island in Loch Shiel where St. Finnan, a disciple of Columba, established himself, and similar missionaries or anchorites set out from Iona to settle in many places on the western coasts.

Iona has no natural features of outstanding interest, though every rocky islet set in the western sea off this enchanted coast cannot fail to be a place of delight. Under suitable conditions, too, the views across the water towards Mull and numerous other islands can be exceedingly beautiful. But such are its associations with the long-distant past that even the modern tourist landing from an excursion steamer in a crowd cannot fail to react to the spirit of the place and feel something, at any rate, of the pilgrim's joy when he sets foot on this hallowed shore.

There are, of course, no buildings which go back within centuries of St. Columba's time. His primitive settlement was rebuilt again and again, and during the ninth century the monastery was more than once burned and destroyed by Norse pirates, who carried off the treasures and slaughtered the monks. In spite of these disasters the monks seem to have returned to their old haunts, but it was not until the twelfth century that the more ambitious buildings, of which some traces remain, were erected. In 1074, St. Margaret, queen of Malcolm III, made gifts for rebuilding the abbey, and in 1202 Reginald, Lord of the Isles, introduced a number of regular Benedictine monks, who gradually absorbed the ancient Celtic establishment. A convent for nuns was founded at the same time.

Of the buildings which remain all are in ruins except the Cathedral, which has recently been repaired. The oldest appears to be St. Oran's Chapel (277), which has been attributed to St. Margaret's day, but the richly carved doorway with its elaborate zigzag mouldings looks half a century later, if we may judge by similar buildings in England, while we should not be surprised in this remote home of tradition to find work of this kind at an even later date. There are considerable remains of the Convent Chapel, but the Cathedral, originally the Abbey Church, is much later, and appears to belong mostly to the fourteenth or fifteenth century, though the pretty little doorway shown in (279) would pass for thirteenth-century work farther south. It is difficult to judge accurately of dates when we have to deal with a local style out of touch with the main trend of development elsewhere. A very curious feature is to be found in the south aisle, formed by low curved buttresses which support the arcade just above the capitals in a very awkward manner (280). It was the custom for centuries to bring the bodies of distinguished persons to this hallowed spot for burial, and it is claimed that forty-eight kings of Scotland, eight kings of Norway, four of Ireland and one of France were buried in Iona. There are a large number of carved slabs from this famous graveyard, mostly dating from the later Middle Ages, but of the three hundred and sixty crosses which are said to have stood here only two remain more or less complete. Of the rest there are a few broken fragments, while others were carried off to the mainland at a later date, like that which we found at Pennygown, or the well-known example at Inveraray. A great number were broken and thrown into the sea by the Protestant reformers. Of the two remaining one stands in front of the Cathedral, and is known as St. Martin's Cross (278), while the other, called Maclean's Cross, stands beside the path on the way to the nunnery. Comparison with the Northumbrian crosses shows that neither of these goes back to the early days of the monastery, and St. Martin's Cross may even be as late as the twelfth century.

We must now leave the holy isle. Our business in this book is with nature rather than with saints or early history, but some slight digression in that direction seemed necessary if we were to visit Iona in the right spirit.

With skye and mull, arran
is the most easily accessible of the larger islands of the west coast. Indeed
it is so easily reached from Glasgow and other populous centres that the lover
of quiet and solitude will do well to avoid the chief ports at Lamlash and
Brodick during the season, especially after the arrival of the boats. But at
Easter he will have most of the place to himself, and, as pointed out elsewhere again and again, there is no better time for roaming over the hills.
The island can be reached either by the boats plying between Ardrossan and
Brodick and Lamlash, or by the Clyde steamers from Gourock, which call
at Loch Ranza on their way to Campbeltown, in Kintyre. The latter route is
through more sheltered waters, and for those who dislike night travelling it
is possible[1] to leave Loch Ranza after a comfortable breakfast and to reach
Glasgow in time to catch the afternoon train to London.

Loch Ranza is prettily situated on an inlet surrounded by high hills, and
would serve as an excellent base for several delightful hill expeditions, but
the hotels at Corrie, about eight miles off on the east coast, and at Brodick,
four or five miles farther on, are better, as they are nearer the finest part of
the mountain ranges. Lamlash possesses a fine harbour, protected by the
conical Holy Island, on which is a cave once occupied by St. Molios, a
disciple of St. Columba. There is a good view of the main ranges of hills
from the ridge between Lamlash and Brodick, but the southern part of the
island is more moorland than mountain, and so need not detain us, though
there are some interesting spots along the coast, notably in the extreme
south, where in April we found the cliffs covered with primroses and other
spring flowers. Thanks to the Gulf Stream, the climate of Arran is very
equable, and severe frosts are rare at sea-level. In sheltered spots it is possible
to grow semi-tropical trees and shrubs with as much success as at Falmouth.

My visit to Arran took place in April 1929, and we divided our stay between
Corrie and Brodick. It was an exceptionally snowless spring, and when we
arrived the hills were entirely bare, though some snow fell before we left.

The hills, which are the chief attraction of the island, are all grouped in
the northern half of it, and some idea of their relative positions may
be gathered from the accompanying sketch-map, in which I have
inserted only the main ridges. None of them reaches a height of even
3,000 feet, Goat Fell, the highest, being only 2,866 feet high, but, in spite of

[1] Or was before the war.

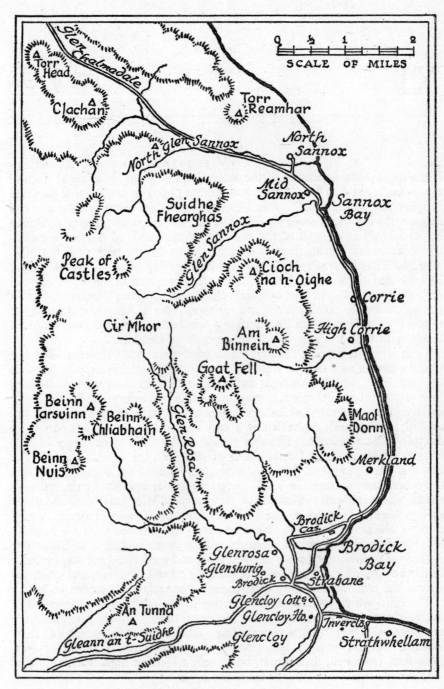

SCALE OF MILES

North-East part of Arran

this, their fine shapes, steep precipices and piled-up rocks give them a wild and stern character which is hardly matched in Scotland outside the Cuillin of Skye.

Two great glens run into the heart of the hills, one from the north and the other from the south, Glen Sannox and Glen Rosa, and they are separated by the very steep saddle which joins the Goat Fell massif to the rugged chain opposite. Glen Sannox opens towards the sea a little north of Corrie, and the banks of the stream where it issues from the glen and tumbles over a rocky bed between steep, tree-clad slopes are pleasant places in which to rest or ramble. Farther up a small mine is rather an eyesore, but is soon passed, and beyond this the wild scenery of the glen is at its best. The path is intermittent, and one has to thread one's way through bogs, which can be very tiresome after wet weather, but it is not necessary to go very far unless the objective is the col at the head, the last part of which provides a very steep climb. Caisteal Abhail, or the Peak of the Castles (2,817 feet), the second highest mountain of Arran, towers up grandly on the right, with its formidable jagged teeth jutting out from the ridge, but all the way up the glen the main feature is the grand pyramid of Cir Mhòr (2,618 feet), the most striking though far from the highest peak of the range (281). It stands just over the saddle at the head of the glen, into which it sends down sheer and forbidding precipices and slabs of bare rock, and is equally impressive from Glen Rosa on the other side (295).

The first really fine day we naturally devoted to the ascent of Goat Fell, *from Corrie* which is best reached by a corrie a mile or so along the Brodick road, and the track leading up a long spur from Brodick is joined at the foot of the final ascent. The summit is a fine one, composed of great piles of granite, especially fine on the Glen Rosa side, where a precipice dips down to the valley far below. The view is very extensive, with glimpses of sea in every direction, backed to the south-east by Ailsa Craig and the Galloway hills, to the west by the long ridge of the Mull of Kintyre, and to the north beyond Bute by the far-off mountains of Argyll. But the chief feature is provided by the wild rocks of the Arran hills themselves. The sharp peak of Cir Mhòr stands up aggressively, though somewhat dwarfed by the bold crags of the Peak of the Castles, crowned with the rock towers to which it owes its name, and with its north-west serrated ridge split into two by the great chasm known as the Witch's Leap (282). To the right a nearer spur of Goat Fell itself rises to a noble peak, which from this point seems almost a rival to Cir Mhòr, though proximity perhaps exaggerates its importance (283). It looks as though it would provide a rough scramble for anyone desirous of reaching the top. The descent to the saddle between the two glens and climb to the summit of Cir Mhòr presents a very formidable appearance, and is probably best left to the experienced rock-climber, but the walk along the ridge which runs north from Goat Fell, forming the eastern wall of Glen Sannox, is both easy walking and most interesting. Although the top of the ridge is fairly smooth, most impressive crags and precipices drop into the valley at one's feet, and their summits are crowned with fantastic piles and bastions of huge granite blocks, which serve as a fitting frame to the view of the shapely peak of Cir Mhòr beyond (284). The granite at the top of these buttresses weathers much in the same way as that familiar to visitors to Cornwall on the cliffs near Land's End. The great squared blocks sometimes look as though built up in courses by some giant hand, but in Arran they are not placed on a cliff a few hundred feet above the sea, but crown a wall 2,000 feet high. Another view of them is given in (292). In this, Beinn Bharrain (2,368 feet) is seen over the shoulder of Cir Mhòr, with Loch Tanna lying at its feet. This hill and its neighbour, Beinn Bhreac (2,333 feet), are the only peaks in Arran which exceed 2,000 feet outside the main group, from which they are separated by the long Glen Iorsa, which opens to the west coast. The walk along the ridge may be continued to the Cioch-na-h'Oighe, or the Pap, a fine rocky peak standing sentinel over the entrance to Glen Sannox (294). Beyond it can be seen the low-lying island of Bute, with the Kyles of Bute and the Clyde estuary beyond. A direct descent over the end of the Cioch looks far too steep to be pleasant, but half a mile short of it a ridge runs out to the east, from which a much more practicable slope leads almost straight to Corrie. This whole round, over Goat Fell and down along the north ridge, is one strongly to be recommended.

The ridge bounding Glen Sannox on the opposite, or north-west, side culminates in a mountain called Suidhe Fhearghas, or the Seat of Fergus (2,081 feet), which is really a continuation of Caisteal Abhail ridge. It can be ascended without much difficulty from the end, and is worth climbing for the view of the jagged teeth of the Castle ridge, backed by Cir Mhòr's shapely peak (293). Whether it could be made a route to the Peak of the Castles itself I am not quite sure, as the chasm of the Witch's Leap appears to bar the way, and we did not have time to explore the position or to find out whether a way round could be found which did not involve going half-way down the mountain and up again.

The best route by which to attack the Peak of the Castles is to take it in the rear. The road to Loch Ranza is followed for nearly four miles from the Corrie Hotel, and then, after crossing the bridge over the stream coming from North Glen Sannox, on the farther side of Suidhe Fhearghas, a moderately dry route can be picked out up to the fine ridge bounding this rather desolate glen. This curves round the head of the glen past a summit called Creag Dhubh in the Ordnance Map, and so leads up to the Castles. There are crags in places along the ridge, but the going along the top is quite good, and though the expedition is not a short one, a ridge-walk is rarely tiring, as the freshness of the air and the interest of the views on both sides seem to act as stimulants. We had started for this walk on a fine morning, but as we reached the ridge a series of little snow showers blew up from the north-west, forcing us to take shelter among the rocks and causing some delay. Fortunately they did not as a rule last long, and the sun came out between them to warm us up and restore brilliance to the landscape. These passing showers, alternating with periods of brilliant sunshine, produced some magnificent effects, which more than compensated us for any temporary

297 Cir Mhòr from Beinn a'Chliabhain

298 Peak of the Castles from Beinn a' Chliabhain

inconvenience or cold while we were waiting for them to pass. As the ridge bent round we had a grand view of Beinn Tarsuinn (2,706 feet), with its top sprinkled with the fresh snow which had just fallen while we were waiting under a rock round the corner (285). The broken ridges on the left of our picture connecting it with the main chain have real mountain character, and one of the little snow showers is seen approaching from the right.

The splendid piles of rock forming the summit of the mountain, to which it owes its name, afford good scrambling, but can be climbed without real difficulty if the right way is found. Their splendid buttresses and tremendous precipices towards the head of Glen Sannox are most impressive, and form a noble frame for Cir Mhòr, which looked particularly fine with a background of sunlit snow-shower sweeping across the country beyond (286). The bare rock precipices of Cir Mhòr are well seen from this point, and beyond, Goat Fell rises also to a fine peak and displays a grand series of steep slabs and gullies on its Glen Rosa face. Beyond is Lamlash harbour, presided over by the sugar-loaf of Holy Island, and far away in the distance the coast of Ayrshire can just be distinguished (287).

As we had been delayed by the snow showers, and progress along the Fhearghas ridge was cut off by the obstacle of the Witch's Leap, it seemed desirable to find a shorter way back than the way by which we had come. We accordingly made our way to the col connecting the Castles with Cir Mhòr. Time did not permit an attempt on that attractive peak from this side, which appears to be the only practicable ascent for anyone but an expert rock-gymnast, and we managed to clamber down into upper Glen Sannox by extraordinarily steep slopes. It was one of those occasions when we were thankful that our way lay downhill and not up, as an ascent by this route would be extremely laborious.

Skirting the base of the Cir Mhòr precipices we made our way down to the valley floor, and so home to Corrie via the bogs of Glen Sannox. We voted this expedition a great success, as the atmospheric effects caused by the passing snow showers provided a wonderful and ever-changing spectacle. It was interesting to compare the photographs taken under these conditions with the far less interesting ones secured on another day when the weather was much more settled and therefore less exciting. I am not one of those full-blooded individuals who deliberately start for the mountain-tops in hopelessly bad weather, but when it is merely doubtful, or if it looks as though an improvement were possible, it is often well worth while to run the risk of a wetting, as the finest effects are usually those which occur when it is clearing up after rain, or in the fine intervals between showers.

After a pleasant sojourn at Corrie we decided to spend our last week at Brodick. The steamer pier and hotels are situated on the south side of the bay, which necessitates an addition of a mile or two to the walks among the big hills, but this is easily compensated for by the view across the bay to the Castle standing in its richly-wooded park, backed by the shapely cone of Goat Fell. In bad or doubtful weather the road along the beach forms an excellent promenade from which to watch the stormclouds sweeping over the hills or stray gleams of light striving to break through the heavy vapours. Two of these weather effects are shown (288 and 289). In the first the heavy cloud is just skimming over the peak of Goat Fell, while a snow shower is drifting across from the entrance to Glen Rosa. In (289) the clouds are beginning to drift away from the tops as a brighter interval approaches, showing the summits whitened by a fresh fall of snow.

In doubtful weather there are pleasant walks to the south away from the hills, and the rest of the island, if less exciting than the north corner, is worth exploration. On a day which was fine and bright, though too windy for a high-level expedition, we walked over to Lamlash by the cliffs, enjoying good views of Holy Island (290), and watching the waves splashing merrily over the rocks, though, of course, Arran is too much encircled by land to enjoy the full splendour of the Atlantic rollers which are such a glorious spectacle in the more exposed portions of our iron-bound western coasts. The return can be made by road, and the panoramic view of the northern mountain ranges from the top of the rise before the descent to Brodick commences is most impressive. The jagged peaks and broken outlines form a fine background to the wide heathery moorland at our feet. Moderate walkers can shorten this expedition by taking the boat from Brodick to Lamlash and walking back. The distance is only about four miles, and the walk should certainly be taken in this direction in order to keep the views in front.

Another expedition we made was to take the boat past Lamlash to Whiting Bay, farther down the coast, whence a motor-coach took us to Kildonan Castle, on the south coast of the island. Here we found cliffs richly decked with primroses and bluebells, and fine reefs of red sandstone rocks jutting out into the sea, interspersed with strange long dykes of volcanic origin.

One of the first expeditions to be made from Brodick is to explore the mountains on the west side of Glen Rosa. For the first three miles or so up the lower part of the glen there is an excellent path, dry and soft to the feet, and a most welcome change after the stones and bogs usually found in a valley of this kind. The path then turns to the north, and rapidly deteriorates as it reaches the upper part of the glen. The main mountain chain on the west side runs south from Cir Mhòr (2,618 feet), the fine peak which dominates the head of this glen very much in the same way as it does Glen Sannox, passes along a ridge called A'Chir, and then splits, sending a spur called Beinn a' Chliabhain (2,141 feet) out to the south-east to form the actual western wall of Glen Rosa. The main chain is then continued by Beinn Tarsuinn (2,706 feet) and Beinn Nuis (2,597 feet), which are separated from Beinn a' Chliabhain by a broad corrie filled with bog.

We turned up to the left from the valley where a stream tumbles down from this bog, threaded our way through this tiresome morass and climbed up on to Beinn Nuis. Thence the walk along the ridge to Beinn Tarsuinn was delightful. There is a good rocky comb along the top, with quite good crags in places, though they do not rival the splendid rock scenery of the Goat Fell or Castles ridges, and the views extended from Cruachan and the hills of Mull in the north to Ireland in the south. From Ben Tarsuinn the

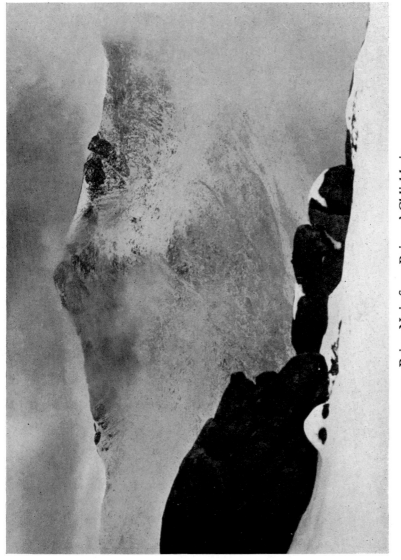

299 Beinn Nuis from Beinn a' Chliabhain

300 Beinn Nuis from Beinn a' Chliabhain

complicated zigzag ridges leading to Cir Mhòr and the Peak of the Castles are well seen (291), but time was slipping away and we had to turn off and follow the interesting ridge of Beinn a' Chliabhain till it sank down to the stream draining the bog, and so down to Glen Rosa.

I now have to describe the day, or rather the hour or two, which stands out in our memories as the most wonderful experience Arran had to show us. It came towards the end of the holiday: the day before had been cold and wet, and there was nothing to be done but to saunter out in mackintoshes between the worst showers and watch the heavy clouds rolling over the hills across the bay. Towards evening there were some slight breaks, through which we caught occasional glimpses of the mountain-tops, and saw that they had been whitened by a considerable fall of snow. We took this as a good sign, as it usually means a shift of the wind towards a northerly quarter, whence the fine weather is to be expected. The morning, however, broke dull and showery, with clouds low on the hills, but the rain left off early and we decided to take a walk up Glen Rosa, in the hope that we might at any rate get some storm-effects between the showers. We were amply rewarded, for the clouds parted as we reached the upper and finest part of the glen, and during some bright sunny intervals we had a glorious glimpse of Cir Mhòr filling the head of the valley to perfection, and supported by the jagged teeth of the Castles ridge beyond (295). With the dark clouds skimming the topmost crags and the rocks gleaming with the fresh-fallen snow we could have imagined ourselves in the Alps, had not the heathery bog and the brown stream tumbling at our feet introduced a more homely note.

The rain had filled up the bog and made further progress along the valley tedious, and as the slope on our left displayed large patches of bracken, a sure sign of drier ground, we turned our steps up the hill, and soon found ourselves mounting the ridge leading to Beinn a' Chliabhain. As we rose the clouds descended again, but as they had cleared once or twice before we pushed on until we came to the snow. A sharp snow shower followed, but as soon as it passed we struggled on to the summit, which we reached in dense mist. For a quarter of an hour or so we sat in the snow, with driving mist hiding everything, but just as we were beginning to think it was hopeless, and were getting up to return, the clouds lightened, and we saw a gleam of sunshine forcing its way through. In a few minutes the clouds parted, and through a rift in the swirling vapours we caught a glimpse of exquisite blue sea and distant hills shining in the sunshine. It is impossible in a photograph to give any suggestion of the beauty of such a colour-effect, but (296) shows Suidhe Fhearghas and a distant hint of the sea, looking noble in its frame of cloud. As we watched, one peak after another revealed itself, gleaming in its snowy mantle and looking several times its real size as the mists swirled round its crags, now hiding and now revealing its summit. Cir Mhòr (297) under these conditions looked more Alpine than ever, and the whole scene was an extraordinary contrast to the snowless ridges over which we had tramped a few days previously. Looking at the Peak of the Castles peering over a sunlit cloud-wreath, with Cir Mhòr's sharp peak piercing the mist (298), it was difficult to realize that we were standing on a hill little over 2,000 feet in height, and that none of these apparent Swiss giants reached 3,000 feet. The snowy hollow below the cloud might have done very well for the snout of a glacier.

In the other direction, Beinn Nuis presented an even more astonishing spectacle, looming through the mists and apparently as inaccessible and as infinitely out of our reach as Mount Everest, though we had tramped over it a few days before without any great exertion (299). Quick changes followed one another in succession, and one splendid spectacle followed on another, until our photographic plates were quickly exhausted. How different Beinn Nuis could look a few minutes afterwards is shown in (300), where the mists have cleared and brilliant sun picks out the dark rocks and snowy slopes against a magnificent background of superb cloud-architecture.

Gradually, however, the grandeur of the effects lessened, and more usual conditions were resumed, and we made our way back to Glen Rosa, congratulating ourselves on our luck in having reached so fine a point of vantage at the right moment. We might have climbed the hill hundreds of times without seeing anything approaching the grandeur of the scene we had just witnessed.

The next day was cold and wet, and was spent packing up for our return home. We had not exhausted the beauties of Arran, but we had at any rate seen these wild hills under the most favourable conditions.

The day of the snow showers on the Peak of the Castles and that of the cloud-effects on Beinn a' Chliabhain will certainly stand out as exceptional manifestations of Nature's noblest aspects, and if we had seen little else during the holiday these two days would have been ample compensation.

Index

References in ordinary type to pages in text. Those in *italics* to the numbers of the illustrations.